The Dilemmas of
GOVERNMENT EXPENDITURE

The Dilemmas of
GOVERNMENT
EXPENDITURE

Essays in political economy by
economists and parliamentarians

ROBERT BACON and **WALTER ELTIS**

TOM WILSON   **JACK WISEMAN**

★   ★   ★

DAVID HOWELL   **DAVID MARQUAND**

JOHN PARDOE

★   ★   ★

RICHARD LYNN

Published by
The Institute of Economic Affairs
1976

First published in 1976 by
THE INSTITUTE OF ECONOMIC AFFAIRS
© The Institute of Economic Affairs 1976

SBN 255 36081-9

Printed in England by
Goron Pro-print Co. Ltd., Lancing, Sussex
Set in Monotype Times Roman 11 on 12 point

Contents

v

The Dilemmas of Government Expenditure

Preface

The *IEA Readings* have been devised to refine the market in ideas by presenting various approaches to a subject in a single volume. It is hoped they will be of special value to teachers and students of economics as well as to laymen who want to know what economists are thinking and writing on the subject that concerns them.

Readings No. 15 has grown out of a Seminar but the verbal discourses have been considerably updated and amplified. Mr Walter Eltis has also brought in his colleague Mr Robert Bacon, and the material under their names is a much fuller statement of the argument they have been deploying. And Mr David Marquand, who was prevented from attending the Seminar owing to absence abroad, has generously gone to some trouble to compile a statement to complete the trio of Parliamentarians from the three parties.

The result is a unique collection of thoughtful analyses of the stubborn task of reducing government expenditure that economists in all schools of thought are coming to accept as a desirable objective. Messrs. Eltis and Bacon of the University of Oxford, Professor Tom Wilson from the University of Glasgow and Professor Jack Wiseman from the University of York approach the subject from varying angles and go to the root of the obstacles to reductions in expenditure that government must face sooner or later. And Professor Richard Lynn analyses the evidence on education.

The three Parliamentarians, among the ablest of the members of their parties, indicate how they see the task of cutting government expenditure: Mr David Howell as a Conservative with experience of office in the 1970-74 Government, Mr John Pardoe as Liberal 'Shadow Chancellor', and Mr Marquand as a member of the Social Democratic wing of the Labour Party.

To varying degrees all six discuss the causes of and cures for excess expenditure and in so doing analyse a wide range of aspects of the subject from government machinery to the changes in policy and the philosophic value-judgements on which they must rest. But more than that: several of them find themselves discussing an aspect that would have seemed cynical or *simpliste* a few years ago or even a few months ago. The expansion in expenditure has reflected far more than inadequate machinery of control, or fallacious philosophic thinking, or out-dated political attitudes: it also reflects, perhaps even more fundamentally, the sheer imperative of using the patronage of government to achieve, consolidate and buttress political power. Some years ago agricultural economists were discussing the subsidy cost incurred by Conservatives to keep agricultural seats; in recent months the discussion has been about the reluctance of the Government to cut expenditure for fear of risking Labour urban seats.

These two examples may seem over-simplified, but they reflect the growing interest of economists in what is called variously the economics of politics, the theory of public choice, the economics of democracy, or other descriptions which indicate that economists are analysing the activities of politicians in the same systematic manner in which they analyse the activities of men in industry with motives of self-preservation and self-advancement. This approach does not imply a judgement about the goodness or badness of politicians or entrepreneurs. It is based on more realistic assumptions than that the activities of politicians could be explained as concerned solely to serve 'the public interest'. A forthcoming Hobart Paper by Professor Gordon Tullock of Virginia, one of the founders of the Virginia School of public choice, and Dr Morris Perlman of the London School of Economics analyses this newer approach of economists more fully.

As a case study in the yield from government expenditure, Professor Lynn reviews the researches into expenditure on the successive stages of education and the poor return revealed by a range of studies. His analysis and conclusions contest the view that government expenditure on 'education' is necessarily desirable and must be maintained and increased on principle in all circumstances.

An aspect of the task of reducing government expenditure that is not considered at length in current debate is the extent to which government services yield private benefits for which the appropriate method of financing is not taxes but prices. The process of controlling expenditure on the 'public' services that have grown in the past century might become more tractable if government did not have to devise machinery for controlling the expansion of private benefits supplied at nil or at less-than-market price. The traumatic pains of 'cutting' expenditure decided after weighing economic imperatives against electoral consequences in the Cabinet Room might be eased if the costs of services for which consumers could pay in the market were made explicit and charges were levied where practicable, so that expenditure was 'cut' by consumers who knew the alternatives they sacrificed rather than by politicians who did not. This subject is discussed in an essay in *Catch '76 . . . ?* and in a forthcoming Hobart Paper incorporating evidence to and an appraisal of the Layfield Report on local government financing.

Interesting observations and propositions made by members of the invited audience at the Seminar are included under the heading 'From the Floor'.

The Institute is grateful to the seven contributors to these Readings who have together combined to produce a volume of stimulating thought of especial value for teachers and students of economics and for people in Westminster, Whitehall, in industry and in the press and broadcasting.

February 1976   ARTHUR SELDON

PART I
The Economists

1. How Growth in Public Expenditure has Contributed to Britain's Difficulties

*ROBERT BACON and WALTER ELTIS**

*This essay is based on a paper delivered at the seminar and subsequently at other seminars. It has been developed into the chapter, 'The Fundamental Problem', in Robert Bacon and Walter Eltis, *Britain's Economic Problem: Too Few Producers*, Macmillan, 1976, which contains an extended version of the argument.

THE AUTHORS

ROBERT BACON has been a Fellow of Lincoln College and Lecturer in Econometrics in the University of Oxford since 1967. He has been a Consultant to UNCTAD and the British Airports Authority.

He is a general editor of *Oxford Economic Papers* and co-author (also with Walter Eltis) of *The Age of US and UK Machinery*, and he has contributed articles to several academic journals.

WALTER ELTIS has been a Fellow of Exeter College and Lecturer in Economics in the University of Oxford since 1963. In 1970 he was Visiting Reader in Economics at the University of Western Australia. He has been a general editor of *Oxford Economic Papers* since 1974 and he was an Economic Consultant to the National Economic Development Office from 1963 until 1966.

He is the author of *Growth and Distribution*, joint editor of *Induction Growth and Trade* and he has published articles on Adam Smith and François Quesnay.

More recently, Robert Bacon and Walter Eltis were joint authors of the 'Declining Britain' articles which appeared in *The Sunday Times* in November 1975.

2

The fundamental ways in which extra-rapid growth of public expenditure cause difficulties for an economy will be explained in this article. The full implications for Britain in particular will then be set out.

It is not obvious to all that public expenditure has grown particularly rapidly in Britain. Such a view can be based, for instance, on official statistics like those which state that the current spending of central and local government increased only from 17·5 per cent of the gross domestic product at constant market prices in 1961 to 21·9 per cent in 1974. Their capital spending merely increased from 4·0 per cent to 4·9 per cent of the gross domestic product in the same period. It might thus appear that the current and capital spending of the public authorities in Britain increased only from 21·5 per cent to 26·8 per cent of the gross domestic product.[1] Spread over 13 years, such an increase should hardly squeeze the remainder of the economy to any significant degree. And OECD data show that public spending increased as much as this in many developed economies.[2]

Such conclusions cannot be drawn from official figures like these. First, they are expressed in constant prices, so they exclude much of the relative price effect—teachers' and civil servants' salaries rising faster than the general price level—which has increased public spending much more than private spending in current money terms. Second, figures like the above exclude transfers from people who produce to those (like pensioners) who do not, so they underrate the extent to which producers have had to finance the increased spending of others. Third, they are based on a division of the economy into public and private sectors rather than market and non-market sectors, which is more relevant to the problems that really matter—inflation, growth and the balance of payments, for marketed output has to provide for the private consumption, investment and export needs of the nation.

How much difference the first two qualifications make is clear

---

[1] *National Income and Expenditure, 1964-74*, Tables 14 and 59, and *1972*, Tables 14 and 50. The totals are expressed as fractions of the gross domestic product at constant factor cost.

[2] For instance, OECD, *National Accounts, 1962-73*.

when figures like those quoted above are contrasted with those of Professor Cedric Sandford and Dr Ann Robinson, whose survey of public expenditure in Britain showed that the combined spending of the central government and local authorities, with pensions and other transfers included, increased from 40·6 per cent to 52·5 per cent of the gross national product in only 10 years—1964 to 1974. With expenditure on financial assets excluded, it increased from 38·0 per cent to 49·3 per cent.[3] It is far more plausible to suppose that increases like these, which show a reduction of about one-fifth in the share of the money national income available to the remainder of the economy, had significant effects.

Moreover, it is the public sector activities which do not provide marketed outputs that put particular pressure on the resources of the remainder of the economy, and spending on these increased still faster than the ratio of public expenditure to the gross national product. The claims on marketed output from outside the market sector increased from 41·4 per cent of marketed output in 1961 to 60·3 per cent in 1974, thus apparently reducing by nearly one-third the proportion of output that market-sector producers could themselves invest and consume. This much larger increase in the ratio of government claims on marketed output resulted from the transfer of workers from producing marketed output to unmarketed public services like administration, and health. This has two distinct effects. First, it reduces the economy's marketed output and, second, it increases what producers must lose out of a diminished total to supply the needs of non-producers. Thus if workers earning £2,000 million are transferred from the market sector to unmarketed public services, marketed output will fall by £2,000 million and the claims of the non-market sector on what remains will rise by £2,000 million (before tax).[4] With the change in public expenditure shown as a share of the national income, the increased claims of £2,000

---

[3] Cedric Sandford and Ann Robinson, 'Public Spending—a feature', *The Banker,* November 1975, pp. 1,241-55.

[4] That Mrs Thatcher has understood this for some time is evident from a speech of 15 September 1975, in which she said:

'The private sector creates the goods and services we need both to export to pay for our imports and the revenue to finance public services. So one must not overload it. Every man switched away from industry and into government will reduce the productive sector and increase the burden on it at the same time'.

million would be shown, but not that £2,000 million less purchasable output was available to meet them, for civil servants' salaries are included in the national income, like those of market-sector workers. The marketed output measure of increased government spending shows such a large increase in Britain because it indicates this dual effect which has been greater in Britain than elsewhere.

The increased taxation needed in Britain

The increase in government claims on marketed output certainly had powerful effects in Britain, and required a big increase in taxation. It will be assumed conservatively that taxation in the market sector had to be raised by 9 per cent of marketed output from 1961 to 1974 to finance the increase in non-market sector claims of 18·9 per cent. The assumed increase is much less than 18·9 per cent for two reasons. First, since non-market sector workers and pensioners pay taxes, it is not necessary to finance their whole cost by taxing the market sector. Second, the British budget was in substantial deficit in 1974 (partly because the world recession was

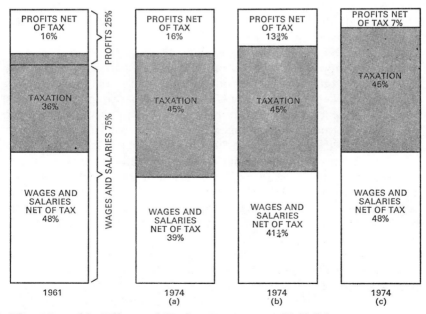

Three Possible Effects of Higher Taxation in 1961-74

5

beginning to have adverse effects on tax revenue) so taxes were not increased as much as expenditure. The increase in taxation in the market sector was a little less than 9 per cent in 1961-74, but it will need to be more than 9 per cent when the economy approaches full employment. Nine per cent is thus sensibly between the actual increase in taxation and what will be needed.

Increased taxation of 9 per cent of marketed output must have strong effects on the economy. The left-hand block of the Chart shows the assumed division of marketed output between profits, wages and salaries, and the government in 1961. It is assumed that 25 per cent of marketed output went to profits before tax (net of capital consumption) and 75 per cent to wages and salaries. Total taxation is assumed to be 36 per cent, and charged on profits and wages and salaries at equal rates, so one-quarter of it was taken from profits and three-quarters from wages and salaries. After tax profit-receivers therefore kept 16 per cent of marketed output (in place of 25 per cent before tax), workers 48 (in place of 75 per cent) and the government obtained the remaining 36 per cent of marketed output. This simplified example can obviously be no more than an approximation to the situation in 1961, but it gives the broad orders of magnitude of the division of marketed output between workers, profit-receivers and the government   .

The three blocks on the right show three possible examples of what could happen when an extra 9 per cent of marketed output has to be taken from those who produce it to enlarge the government's share of marketed output to 45 per cent. In (a), profit-receivers keep 16 per cent of marketed output as in 1961, and the extra 9 per cent the government takes comes wholly from workers and salary-earners. They therefore receive 39 per cent of marketed output after all taxes in place of 48 per cent. This result could come about if the government levied the entire extra taxation of 9 per cent on workers and salary-earners while the distribution of incomes before tax remained as it was, or if it raised taxes equally on wages and profits, but businessmen could pass profits taxes on to the consumer. Then profits net of all taxes would be the same as before and the entire extra cost of the non-market sector would be paid by workers and salary-earners through higher taxes and their lower share of total incomes in the market sector.

In block (b), profits and wages lose equal shares to pay the extra 9 per cent, so profits pay for one-quarter of it, and wages and salaries the other three-quarters. Net-of-tax profits therefore fall from 16 per cent of marketed output in 1961 to $13\frac{3}{4}$ per cent in 1974, while wages and salaries fall from a net-of-tax 48 per cent to a net-of-tax $41\frac{1}{4}$ per cent. This could come about through equal tax increases on wages and profits, or through different tax increases and compensating changes in the distribution of incomes.

Block (c) shows the possibility that corresponds most closely to what happened in Britain in 1961 to 1974. The whole of the government's extra 9 per cent to raise its share of marketed output to 45 per cent is taken from net-of-tax profits, which therefore fall from 16 per cent of marketed output in 1961 to 7 per cent in 1974. With profits paying the whole extra cost of the larger non-market sector, workers and salary-earners continue to receive 48 per cent of it after all taxes. Again, this situation could come about in two broad ways. First, the government could levy all the additional taxes it needed on profits or incomes derived from them while the distribution of incomes remained unchanged. Alternatively much of the additional taxation could be levied on wages and salaries in the first instance, but if workers had the power to pass these taxes on, profits could end up losing the whole 9 per cent. Workers can pass taxes on by causing exceptional wage inflation that leads to a squeeze on profit margins, either because prices and incomes policies, which impose lower profit margins on companies, are introduced to control inflation, or because the exchange rate is not lowered in line with domestic inflation, with the result that international competition squeezes profit margins.

The extra 9 per cent taxation of marketed output could thus cut net-of-tax wages and salaries by 9 per cent of marketed output (a), or net-of-tax profits by 9 per cent (c), or both together (b). These may all have significant effects, and something corresponding quite closely to one of them must happen, for an extra 9 per cent of marketed output must be taken from either profits or wages and salaries or both together.

If it is predominantly wages and salaries that are squeezed, workers' consumption has to fall from 48 to 39 per cent of marketed output during the 13-year transition period. If marketed output rose rapidly at the same time, workers' private net-of-tax incomes could fall from 48 to 39 per cent of this and still grow very fast indeed in absolute terms. Thus if marketed output per head rose at a West European rate of 5 per cent a year during the 13 years, the *private* consumption of workers and salary-earners could rise 53·2 per cent or 3·3 per cent per annum during this period. A reduction in the rate of increase of living standards, in terms of private consumption, from 5 to 3·3 per cent a year for 13 years would be enough to divert the necessary extra resources to the non-market sector. It is because some economies have had growth rates in marketed output like these that they have been able to achieve a rapid transfer of resources into the non-market sector and a high rate of increase of private consumption per head at the same time. Consider in contrast a similar transfer of resources to the non-market sector with the British rate of growth of marketed output per head of about $2\frac{1}{2}$ per cent per annum. Here private net-of-tax incomes can grow only 12 per cent in the 13-year transition period, or at 0·9 per cent per annum. To divert resources to higher social spending, workers can be expected to accept much more readily a reduction in the rate of growth of private consumption from 5·0 to 3·3 per cent for 13 years than from 2·5 to 0·9 per cent per annum, which could lead to markedly more frustration and union militancy.

Does social spending reflect worker preferences?

There would, of course, be no adverse response to such a diversion of resources if the increased social spending was a direct and exact response to workers' preferences. There are two conceivable ways in which this could come about. Social spending decisions could be taken through parliament, and the policies the government of the day implemented could in theory reflect the preferences of the great majority of the electorate, and therefore of most workers and salary-earners. If they were really aware of the costs of policies when they voted for them, the increased taxation would be part of what they voted for. The electorate should then expect a much slower rate of growth of private net-of-tax incomes than of aggregate output, and there should then be no attempt to get extra wage and salary increases to compensate for higher taxation. Alternatively, a decision to increase social spending relative to private spending could be taken rationally as part of an incomes policy negotiated nationally. A central trade union leadership with the power to commit member unions and the rank and file could agree to exercise wage restraint if the government increased social spending much faster than the national product. If either of these conditions could be met, even a slow-growing economy could divert resources rapidly into the non-market sector without a wages explosion, and achieve an orderly 13-year transition to the situation illustrated in block (a) where the government takes 45 per cent of marketed output in place of 36 per cent, and workers bear the entire costs.

But if neither set of conditions can be met, workers will not necessarily acquiesce in a reduction in the rate of increase of private consumption per head from 2·5 to 0·9 per cent for 13 years. Only the Scandinavian countries have the machinery to bargain about the 'social wage' nationally and trade union leadership that can commit the rank and file. Other countries must therefore rely on their parliaments to allocate resources between private and social spending. For this mechanism to give a result that reflects the true wishes of the people, the costs of social policies must be made clear at election time. If political parties pretend they can increase both private and public consumption at rapid rates, they may be voted into office and then dismay the electorate when the bills have to be paid. The electorate as workers and members of trade unions may then all too easily respond by refusing to accept the bills which were not what they voted for. To refuse to pay taxes is impractical, because this can rapidly result in the sequestration of property and imprisonment, but obtaining wage and salary increases which make up for extra taxation is often perfectly possible—at least for a time.

This is almost precisely what happened in Britain in 1961 to 1974. Lack of knowledge by the people at election time of the extra tax costs of higher social spending that *they themselves* would have to pay, or disappointment at the failure of the 'social wage' to rise significantly in *output* terms, or inconsistency between votes in favour of the 'social wage' and industrial action in favour of private consumption could all help to explain the push for higher pay to offset higher taxes. The likeliest explanation is that the full tax costs of social spending programmes, local government reorganisation (which has led to soaring local authority rates) and so on were never made clear enough. The British people therefore voted for higher social spending and then set off rapid wage inflation when they realised to their surprise that they were expected to pay for it.

Monetarists would not allow that frustrated workers can set off rapid inflation without government co-operation, for they believe that workers could only push up wages rapidly if governments increased the money supply at similar rates. They would expect prices to be stable if the government increased the money supply

9

only as much as the long-term growth rate, whether taxation on workers' consumption rose or fell. But they would concede that frustrated workers could raise money wages rapidly at first until lack of growth of the money supply began to bite. With money wages rising and the money supply held back, unemployment would mount, and it is therefore extra unemployment that workers' frustration due to rising taxation would cause. This analysis is surely correct; and it means that the argument can be set out more generally. If workers are frustrated by rising taxation, *either* inflation will accelerate (if the money supply is allowed to expand), *or* unemployment will rise (if the money supply is controlled).[5] The range of options will therefore deteriorate, and governments will be faced with the choice of *either* more inflation than in the past, *or* more unemployment, *or,* as a third alternative, tougher incomes policies with stronger sanctions. Such countries are only too likely to end up with the stagflation from which many have recently suffered.

In Britain, the workers certainly raised money wages more rapidly when taxation increased. This means that the increased cost of non-market expenditure was not met, as in principle it could have been, through a 9 per cent reduction in the share of marketed output going to wages and salaries. The case where profits net of all taxes fall by 9 per cent of marketed output appears to correspond most closely to what happened in Britain. What are the full implications?

The implications for investment

If the entire extra 9 per cent of marketed output that the government needs must be found from net-of-tax profits, they must fall by over one-half, from 16 per cent to 7 per cent of marketed output. Businesses finance much of their investment by ploughing back profits, so if they fall by over one-half after tax, investment will be severely threatened. Companies have two possible additional sources of finance (apart from the government). They can issue equity shares

---

[5] In technical terms monetarists would describe this deterioration of options as an increase in the 'natural' rate of unemployment, i.e. in the unemployment rate at which prices are stable. (Professors Milton Friedman and David Laidler, *Unemployment versus Inflation?* Occasional Paper 44, IEA, 1975.) It would be a prediction of the theory we are putting forward that the increase in the 'natural' rate of unemployment (or rightward movement of the Phillips curve) throughout the world since 1960 would be partly explained by the inverse of 'the increase in marketed output per worker *less* the rate of diversion of marketed output per worker to the non-market sector', in the various countries.

on the stock exchange, and borrow on fixed interest. But equity shares cannot be sold on acceptable terms where profits are falling in relation to marketed output and profit expectations are depressed, as they will be if net-of-tax earnings fall by one-half (as a share of marketed output) in 13 years. In such a situation, firms will be able to invest much more than their retained earnings only if they are prepared to borrow heavily on fixed interest.

The difficulty with fixed interest borrowing on a large scale is that it increases the risk of bankruptcy, or at any rate takeover by creditors who generally change managements that cannot pay the interest they have contracted. A firm which finances investment wholly from its profits can continue to produce so long as it continues to earn profits. A company which has to pay interest to outsiders equivalent to half its profits in normal times will be unable to meet its interest costs from profits if they fall 60 or 70 per cent. If it also lacks reserves so that it finds the payment of interest an embarrassment, the banks and insurance companies which lent the money might decide to put in other managers and the managers who borrowed imprudently will then become unemployed with a record of recent failure. Bankruptcy would follow a prolonged inability to meet interest commitments. In contrast, a fall in profits of 60 or 70 per cent in a recession would leave managements relatively safe from outside interference if all the money they had used to finance investment came from ploughed-back profits.

Because of the risks involved in borrowing on fixed interest terms, companies prefer to finance a high proportion of their investment from retained earnings. A company that considered it sound financial policy to finance at least two-thirds of its investment in this way would be able to borrow 50p on fixed interest terms for each £1 of its own profits it reinvested, so its investment would be *at most* one-and-a-half times its retained earnings. A second company, prepared to take bigger risks, might willingly borrow £1 for each £1 of retained earnings ploughed back, while a third might borrow only up to 25p for each £1 it reinvested. While the ratios differ, investment is limited to some multiple of the retained earnings ploughed back in all the three cases.[6]

---

[6] In technical terms, it is being suggested that there are upper limits to the gearing ratios that firms are prepared to use. The gearing ratio limit will then set a ceiling to the amount of fixed interest debt firms are prepared to incur, and investment will be at most retained earnings times a multiple which depends on the maximum tolerable gearing ratio.

If net-of-tax profits fall from 16 to 7 per cent of marketed output, the investment that firms can finance by reinvesting their profits will fall drastically, and companies will also find it prudent to borrow less because their safe borrowing levels are multiples of the amounts they can plough back. If most companies are well below their prudent borrowing limits, this will hardly affect aggregate investment, for they will be able to borrow the money to finance investment they can no longer reinvest from profits. But if most companies are at or close to their limits, the reduction in internal finance for investment will also cut the amount it is safe to borrow on fixed interest terms, so investment will be doubly reduced.

In the economy as a whole some companies will be in the first situation; they will be able safely to make up through borrowing the finance they no longer obtain from profits. But there will also be many companies already borrowing as much as they think sound, and they will not be able to make good the shortfall in retained earnings by borrowing more. Indeed they will have to borrow less than in the past if they put less of their own profits into their businesses each year.

There are always likely to be some such companies; they will have to invest less where net-of-tax profits fall. If most companies are rather close to their safe borrowing limits, the majority will invest less. The result will be a large fall in investment in the market sector as a share of marketed output. A fall in retained earnings of one-half would reduce investment by about one-half if all the companies in the economy were close to their debt limits. Because many are likely to be below their limits in any given year, the fall in investment could generally be expected to be markedly less than one-half where undistributed profits fall one-half after tax—but there is no doubt that aggregate investment will fall as a share of marketed output.

If employees resist squeezes, why not employers?

Workers are liable to resist strongly where they are squeezed, so that they can often make good, through higher money wages, any reduction in their standard of living due to higher taxation and higher prices. Why cannot companies do the same? In theory they can, and there is much evidence that profits taxes often are passed on.[7]

---

[7] Peter Mieszkowski, 'Tax Incidence Theory: the Effects of Taxes on the Distribution of Income', *Journal of Economic Literature,* Vol. VII, December 1969, gives a survey of the evidence.

But there is also evidence since 1960 (certainly in Britain) that the main effect of higher public spending has been to squeeze net-of-tax profits and therefore investment rather than net-of-tax wages and salaries. Fundamentally this must be because, in some countries, companies now lack the power of trade unions to pass taxes on for the reasons outlined above (p. 7).

A recent statistical study has arrived at precisely the result that increases in public expenditure and therefore taxation have had strong adverse effects on private sector investment. Mr David Smith, formerly of the Bank of England, has published a cross-section study of investment, public spending (measured conventionally), inflation and growth for 19 countries in the period 1961-72; his conclusions included the following proposition:

'Until further, and better, estimates can be provided by others the author would like to suggest that, as a simple rule of thumb to concentrate the mind, it be assumed that each 5 per cent increase in the share of national disposable income absorbed by direct state consumption (on the narrow definition excluding transfer payments) implies a 1·0 per cent drop in the growth rate'.

It drops primarily because '. . . each increase in the narrow definition of state consumption of 1·0 per cent of NDI [net domestic incomes] produces a 0·94 per cent drop in the ratio of investment to NDI'.[8] Mr Smith's statistical results are completely in harmony with the analysis presented here. Higher state consumption must squeeze net-of-tax profits or wages and salaries as a share of marketed output. In so far as it squeezes profits, and this is perhaps what it is now most likely to squeeze in many countries, it will also squeeze investment, because many companies will consider it imprudent to borrow on fixed interest terms the finance they can no longer find from their profits, especially if net-of-tax profits are falling, and many are particularly pessimistic about future profitability.

There is one further direction from which private-sector finance for investment could come. Foreign companies could conceivably provide the investment that the domestic firms cannot or will not finance. This possibility can be dismissed at once. Falling net-of-tax profits with workers pushing up wages rapidly to preserve their own

---

[8] David Smith, 'Public Consumption and Economic Performance', *National Westminster Bank Quarterly Review*, November 1975.

net-of-tax earnings would discourage foreign capital. If conditions
became bad enough, money might come in from foreign governments
for charitable reasons, but multinational companies will seek to
withdraw as much capital as they can from a country with sharply
falling net-of-tax profits and rampant wage inflation, and all the
ensuing social and industrial conflict.

Inadequate investment and structural unemployment

It is therefore overwhelmingly likely that if net-of-tax profits are
squeezed as a result of an increase in the proportion of marketed
output taken by government, investment will fall too. The implications are of profound importance, for inadequate investment can
all too easily lead to structural unemployment. It is a well-known
principle of economic theory that if output can be raised 5 per cent
a year and £2 of capital is needed to produce £1 worth of output per
annum, 10 per cent of output must be invested each year.[9] This
fundamental proposition is illustrated in the Table.

**The relationship between growth of marketed output and investment
requirements where £2 of capital is needed to produce £1 of output
per annum:**

	Possible output	Capital required	Investment needed
Economy A: 5 per cent growth			
Year 1	100	200	10
Year 2	105	210	10·5
Year 3	110·25	220·5	11·02
Economy B: 2 per cent growth			
Year 1	100	200	4
Year 2	102	204	4·08
Year 3	104·04	208·08	4·16

In Economy A where there is 5 per cent growth, capital has to be
raised from 200 to 210 between Years 1 and 2 if output is to be
raised from 100 to 105, and this can only be achieved by investing

[9] This is an application of the Harrod-Domar formula which states that a
country's long-term share of investment must equal *the rate of growth* times
the capital needed to produce a unit of output.

10 per cent of the first year's output. All *net* investment is an addition to the capital stock, so investment of 10 raises the capital stock by the necessary 10 from 200 to 210.

Now suppose an economy in these conditions has the technological potential to raise its market sector output 5 per cent a year because it can raise output per worker 4 per cent a year and employment 1 per cent a year. If it needs £2 of capital to produce £1 of output, it will have to invest 10 per cent of market-sector output like Economy A. Imagine that because of a profits squeeze it invests only 4 per cent of its output like Economy B. Its capital stock will then grow only 2 per cent a year from 200 to 204 in one year and 208 in two, and so on, like Economy B's. With this slow growth of capital, output will be able to advance only from 100 to 102 to 104, instead of from 100 to 105 and 110 like Economy A's. But if output grows by only 2 per cent a year and output per worker rises 4 per cent a year, employment must fall 2 per cent a year. Hence if an economy with the growth potential of A limits itself to B's investment, it will have only B's 2 per cent rate of growth, so its 4 per cent productivity growth rate will lead to a 2 per cent loss of jobs each year. Thus in this simplified example, A can have a 5 per cent rate of growth and a 1 per cent increase in jobs if it invests 10 per cent, and it will enjoy only a 2 per cent rate of growth, and it will lose 2 per cent of its jobs each year if it invests just 4 per cent.

There are two true ways and one false way out of this trap. The false way out for the unfortunate country is to raise its rate of growth of productivity from 4 to 6 per cent without investing more or cutting the capital costs required to produce a unit of output. With only 4 per cent of output invested its rate of growth will still be B's 2 per cent. Therefore with 2 per cent output growth and 6 per cent growth of output per worker, 4 per cent of its labour force will become redundant each year instead of 2 per cent. These workers will either languish in idleness, or be absorbed into the non-market sector, which would then require still higher taxation and squeeze profits yet again so that even the 4 per cent investment rate of Economy B would be difficult to sustain.

In contrast, a true way out of the trap is to raise investment to 10 per cent of marketed output. It could then grow at 5 per cent like Economy A. If this must be financed largely from profits, the non-market sector may need to be reduced in size relative to the market sector to allow taxes to be cut, and the share of profits net of tax to rise. Another true way out of the trap would be to drop the rule that £2 of capital is needed to produce £1 of output a year. If rising output from the existing capital stock could be achieved, the case shown below would be a possibility.

	Possible output	Capital required	Investment needed
Economy C: 5 per cent growth *with falling capital requirements*			
Year 1	100	200	4
Year 2	105	204	4·20
Year 3	110·25	208·20	4·41

Economy C, which solves all the problems, has A's 5 per cent rate of growth and B's 4 per cent share of investment. It accomplishes this by steadily cutting the capital required to produce a unit of output, and the capital required to equip a worker.

Any economy would find it marvellous if it could obtain what C achieves—extra growth without having to pay for it. In principle, with rapid technical progress, the capital cost of growth could rise (economists call this *capital-using* technical progress) or fall (*capital-saving* technical progress) or stay the same (*neutral* technical progress). C is an example of capital-saving technical progress. It can happen, but historically technical progress has been capital-using as often as it has been capital-saving. Marx based his predictions on the belief that technical progress would always be capital-using, which he assumed because of what happened in the first century after the industrial revolution, so he predicted that capital-output ratios would continuously rise and cause growing technological unemployment. There will also be growing technological unemployment if technical progress is neutral (i.e. the amount of capital needed to produce a unit of output neither rises nor falls) and the share of investment falls because profits are squeezed. If profits have to be squeezed and investment falls continuously, capitalism will be saved only if technical progress is capital-saving, the precise opposite of Marx's assumption, so that as with Economy C, 5 per cent growth can be attained with only 4 per cent investment. This is a great deal to hope for and an economy will be extremely fortunate if it happens. Britain has not managed to achieve it for reasons which will be discussed when the relevance of the argument to the country's problems is considered below (pp. 18-19).

Wage inflation or structural unemployment

An economy can in principle suffer from two kinds of problem if the ratio of non-market expenditure is raised significantly. First, if the share of output received by workers and salary-earners is reduced to provide the extra resources the government requires, wage inflation may accelerate, or alternatively if the money supply is controlled, more unemployment will be needed to check it. If net-of-tax profits are reduced instead of wages, investment will suffer to an extent depending on how near companies are to their borrowing limits, and if investment falls the rate of growth of productive capacity is likely to fall and technical progress will produce growing redundancies instead of extra output. The only way of avoiding this consequence is to achieve capital-saving technical change—and this will not happen easily.

The increase in non-market expenditure in Britain has produced both kinds of adverse effect. Attempts were made to finance extra non-market spending at the expense of workers' consumption, and deductions from pay-packets rose by about the 9 per cent of marketed output needed for this purpose, so the economy could in principle have achieved a transition where workers bore the entire cost. But workers did not acquiesce, so wage inflation accelerated, unemployment rose and incomes policies had to be made increasingly strict. Through the extra inflation they caused, workers managed to pass the bulk of extra taxation on to companies, which ended up having to pay for the larger non-market sector. Companies have responded by investing less. With its faster productivity growth rate, the country has needed more investment, not less, to maintain employment in the market sector. So the economy has also suffered from declining market sector employment, which started to decline rapidly long before the onset of the world recession. Britain is therefore suffering both from growing structural unemployment, and from incomes policies that have to be tougher or from unemployment that has to be higher than before to contain inflation. And the adverse trends, if left unchecked, will continue so that structural unemployment will become still higher and workers still more discontented.

Why the failure to achieve capital-saving technical progress?

That is how Britain's crisis has come about. The one question that still requires an answer is why the country has failed to achieve the capital-saving technical progress that would have allowed it to grow faster and invest less at the same time. It can be supposed that industrialists base their choice of plant on the relative costs of labour and capital. The cost of employing labour has risen sharply in Britain since 1961. Taxes on employment to finance improved social security benefits have risen dramatically, and money wages have also risen considerably relative to product prices. But the cost of capital has risen too, because when firms approach their borrowing limits it is to be expected that they will attach a high notional cost to the use of extra capital. Hence the costs of capital and labour have both risen sharply, but the cost of labour may have risen more. If it has, firms may have biased their investment in the capital-using and labour-saving direction—thus accentuating the problem.

But it would still have been solved if Britain had been able to achieve rapid capital-saving productivity growth. This is the solution of those who see Britain's weaknesses as the result of failures by workers and managements to achieve adequate productivity growth. It will be evident from what has been said that merely to have raised productivity faster would not have solved Britain's problem. Higher labour productivity with *the same capital requirements to produce a unit of output* would have *increased* the investment needed to prevent growing structural unemployment in the market sector. What was needed was higher productivity and *a fall in the investment required to produce a unit of output* at the same time. The first of these can be called curing *overmanning*, and the second (where more output is produced from the same plant) curing *under-production*. Britain suffers from both in, for instance, the motor-car industry,[10] but *under-production* is the fault that is crucially relevant.

The Think Tank listed several reasons why the British motor-car industry obtains less output from the same plant than firms on the Continent. They cited examples of similarly equipped assembly lines producing 75 per cent and 120 per cent more on the Continent. They said that British assembly lines move more slowly and so produce less output per unit of capital. They also suffer more interruptions

---

[10] Central Policy Review Staff, *The Future of the British Car Industry*, HMSO, 1975.

from stoppages. Of the total production so lost, manufacturers were said to attribute 40 per cent to shortages of materials due to external disputes, or poor stock control where necessary materials and components are not ordered in time. Finally, British plants lost twice as many hours through mechanical breakdowns even though the industry employs 80 per cent more workers on maintenance.[11]

If these faults apply to many British industries, as they probably do—it is unlikely that the car industry is unique—much under-production is evidently due to failures by management and labour on the shop floor. There is relatively little that governments can do to put such defects right. But there is one aspect of under-production where governments may be able to give a little assistance. The utilisation of plant can obviously be improved if output grows more rapidly, for this would allow items of equipment used for only a few hours a week to be used for longer. Moreover, with faster growth of demand, workers can raise productivity without losing their jobs. Therefore, if Britain could achieve a faster rate of growth by other means, such as investing more and allocating more economic resources to activities that are directly productive, the output of existing plant should rise where it is not inefficiency due to labour and managements that is holding it back, so there could be a double benefit in some industries. The world's fastest-growing economies have the lowest capital costs of growth, which makes their growth easier to sustain. If Britain could escape from the vicious circle of slow growth, low demand for the output of particular items of plant and an industrial environment where extra efficiency often causes redundancies so that incentives to improve productivity are minimal, much might be achieved. Progress might be made to cure Britain's problem of under-production if governments started to solve some of the economy's other problems.

Government action on the profits and investment squeezes

Governments will therefore need to tackle the profits squeeze, and the investment squeeze it has caused. Here the Left's position is absolutely clear-cut. It accepts that there has been a profits squeeze and welcomes it, but recognises that the consequent squeeze on

---

[11] CPRS, *ibid.*

investment is regrettable. With capitalism unviable as it is in Britain in the middle 1970s, the Left knows that the state will have to ensure that there is enough capital to provide jobs, for without profits companies simply cannot.

A non-Left government which wished to restore the economy would need to reverse the sequence of events which led to the profits and investment squeeze of 1961-74. If the government's requirements fell back from 45 to 36 per cent of marketed output, 9 per cent extra could go to net-of-tax wages or profits, and both would probably gain. This should lessen the pressure for increased money wages, and the temptation to moderate workers to elect militants. In so far as company profits benefited from lower taxation, there would be more internal finance for investment and more willingness to borrow; and with rising profits the stock exchange should become more buoyant, enabling fast-growing companies to obtain equity finance on acceptable terms. In addition, with all these favourable trends for profitability, international investment should again be attracted to Britain to supplement domestic resources.

Some economists have failed to observe the disintegration of the economy because in their theoretical approach aggregate saving determines investment. They do not believe collapsing company saving will cause difficulties provided that personal saving rises to take its place. But if all the saving is done in the personal sector, and the investment has to be undertaken by companies which have no profits, trouble must result. The companies will not invest without profits, and the personal saving will have to be lent to the government (for who would wish to lend directly to unprofitable companies?), which will then have to find a way of passing it on to the company sector. This must involve *dirigiste* Left policies, so these are inevitable if saving is predominantly personal, and companies are unprofitable.

Other economists believe that the government should continue to take extra resources from the market sector and raise taxation to pay for them, because that is the direction in which a civilised community should progress. Many who hold these views also believe that the government should avoid *dirigiste* Left policies like import controls and direct state intervention in investment decisions because such interference is inefficient. They consider the market more efficient and believe it should take private-sector investment decisions. But with growing public expenditure and taxation, profits can become so low that the market sector will generate insufficient investment.

The market will not then be able to allocate the nation's investment resources efficiently because there will be insufficient profits to allow it to function as it should.

Moreover, with workers discontented, devaluations will produce accelerating inflation instead of balance-of-payments equilibrium. If growing public expenditure and accompanying taxation is allowed to reduce profits to the point where a market economy cannot function effectively, only *dirigiste* Left policies can prevent chaos. So these economists, and they are numerous, must choose. They can support the allocation of investment resources through the market, or they can support policies of higher public spending, but not both.

And the British people must decide, either to strengthen the market sector so that it can function effectively, or to support the Left. Once the choice is made, the policies chosen must be continued long enough to allow the structural balance of the economy to be restored.

2. The Impact of Inflation and Economic Growth

TOM WILSON

Adam Smith Professor of Political Economy,
University of Glasgow

THE AUTHOR

TOM WILSON, OBE, MA, PhD, was born in 1916 and educated at the Queen's University, Belfast (BA, 1938), the University of London (PhD, 1940), and the University of Oxford (MA, 1946). He was a Fellow of University College and Lecturer, University of Oxford, 1946-58. He has been Adam Smith Professor of Political Economy at the University of Glasgow since 1958.

Professor Wilson's publications include *Inflation* (1961), *Planning and Growth* (1964), and *Pensions, Inflation and Growth* (1974); and contributions to *Economic Journal, Economica, Review of Economic Studies*, etc. He was General Editor of the *Oxford Economic Papers,* 1948-58.

Is public expenditure in Britain too high relatively to national output? A strong body of opinion would support this view. Others would reject it although some would concede that the *speed* at which public expenditure has grown in recent years has been excessive. How can we assess these conflicting views?

I BASIC PRINCIPLES

A good many years ago, Colin Clark maintained that taxation should not exceed about a quarter of GNP, but most developed nations have gone far beyond this limit. Japan has been the outstanding exception, and her relatively low level of public expenditure has presumably made it easier for her to sustain a high level of investment and a fast rate of growth. Growth, as conventionally measured, is not however the only objective that private people or their governments may wish to pursue, and it is better to recognise at the outset that there is no 'right' relationship between public expenditure and output, or between taxation and output, that can be held to apply to all countries.[1] Even for a single country, such as Britain, economists cannot prescribe a figure that is scientifically 'right'. For we are dealing here with a question of 'trade-offs'—the exchange of some additional gains from government spending for gains from private spending. It is only to be expected that these 'trade-offs' will be viewed in a different light by different people. There are two obvious reasons why this should be so.

First, there are differences in the empirical assessments that people may make of the sacrifice that will be entailed under one heading in order to obtain gains under another. The old and inconclusive debate about incentives and taxation is a familiar example. That is to say people may hold different views about the facts of any particular situation and about the consequences that stem from them. We cannot expect to have a clear-cut answer even to the scientific question. It is necessary to add, however, that these differences about empirical matters could be reduced by better and more carefully analysed information. It is one of the duties of responsible

---

[1] I do not wish to imply that Colin Clark was claiming that there is such a unique figure. He was talking about an upper limit and his 25 per cent indicated the region in which he thought that limit lay.

politicians—and of professional economists—to do what they can to make such information as widely available as possible. The facts about public administration are relevant here as well as the statistics. For we must ask whether the procedure for decision-making is such as to foster rational choice. We cannot even take it for granted that relative increases in public expenditure will always be seen to mean relative decreases in take-home pay. Then, secondly, differences of opinion may reflect differences in basic value-judgements. Differences may emerge even if the same views about the facts are held by disinterested people who are free from bias. The third source of difference is the rather obvious one that people are by no means free from bias.

Government expenditure too low or too high?

It is not surprising, therefore, that opinions differ a good deal about the desirable proportion of public expenditure to national output over a considerable range. There will be zones at either extreme, however, where the majority in favour of more or less would grow very large and strong. If public expenditure were so low that important public services were being provided on a miserable scale, we should expect strong support for an increase. For one can envisage a situation in which private affluence was accompanied by public squalor without necessarily agreeing that that is a fair description of the situation in practice. One can envisage easily enough the opposite extreme also, and it can scarcely be doubted that we have been rapidly approaching this second zone in recent years with the result that an increasing number of informed people appear to be of the opinion that public expenditure is too high.

The basic question here relates to consistency. It is quite possible in principle that people might prefer to have more goods and services supplied outside the market by the state. They might also prefer to have more incomes paid in the form of state benefits and less in return for contributions to production. If these are indeed their choices and if the choices are made with open eyes and a full awareness of the consequences, both long-run and short, have economists any valid grounds for criticism? Perhaps not—but we can insist that it would be folly to proceed with policies that raised the relative importance of public expenditure if the consequences were inadequately perceived or neglected. Will people work as hard to obtain more public goods as to obtain more private goods? Will they show the same enterprise? Will it, indeed, be possible for them to do so in view of organisational differences? Will they save just as much? Will they abate their claims on the more restricted supply of private goods? Will they appreciate that this supply will be restricted not only because a higher proportion of any given level of output will be taken by the state but also because total output is likely to grow more slowly over time?

In short, some people may try to have it both ways and thus ignore the need for choice. Or they may hope that the other fellow—the rich fellow—can be made to pay. Here we are touching on a persistent and dangerous myth which undoubtedly clouds the issue and reduces the likelihood of rational choice. Most people might agree that there are many inequitable features in our society, but the error lies in supposing that a large sum would be made available for redistribution by despoiling the rich. The Government itself has admitted that 'if no taxpayer were left with more than £5,000 per annum after tax, this would increase the yield by only about 6 per cent'. That is to say, the yield of *income tax* would be increased by only 6 per cent. Or total tax revenue would be raised by about $2\frac{1}{4}$ per cent, equivalent to something like 1 per cent of GNP.

Undoubtedly there has been a marked strengthening of the opinion that public expenditure in Britain has been growing too rapidly and is now too high at its current level of something like three-fifths of GNP.[2] Both public expenditure and GNP are at factor cost. With expenditure and taxation so very high, public finance raises some of the most important questions of choice in economics. But I think it is not untrue to say that this fact has been inadequately recognised in the teaching of economics. Most of the economic textbooks devote much attention to the choices of individuals and firms as expressed through the market and to the warping of the pattern of expenditure by 'imperfect competition'. But the determination of the total level of public expenditure and its allocation between uses have received little attention, although the problems involved are probably very much more important than those posed by so-called 'imperfect competition'.

---

[2] Official estimate given in *Public Expenditure to 1979-80*, Cmnd. 6393, February 1976, p. 1. On the same page it is recorded that: 'In the last three years public expenditure has grown by nearly 20 per cent in volume, while output has grown by less than 2 per cent'.

II INTERNATIONAL COMPARISONS

Public expenditure is high in Britain but we must recognise at the outset that it is also high in other developed countries. If we express total public expenditure as a percentage of GNP, we obtain the following results for 1973: Germany, 38½ per cent; Italy, 40 per cent; the Netherlands, 48 per cent; France, 37 per cent; Sweden, 50 per cent; Japan, 21½ per cent; UK, 41 per cent. The British figure was not, therefore, so abnormally high as is sometimes supposed.

These figures relate to total public expenditure on goods and services, social transfers, subsidies, debt interest, etc., by all forms of government but do not include expenditure by nationalised industries. The figures for the foreign countries are at market prices because this is how they are presented in the OECD publication from which they are derived. For comparability, British figures are also at market prices. That is to say, indirect taxes less subsidies are included in the prices for expenditure on goods and services and in the total figures for GNP. Unfortunately these estimates at market prices can be somewhat misleading, for indirect taxes (less subsidies) fall much more heavily on personal consumption than on the goods and services bought by government.

If we are interested in the claim on real resources, it is better to use estimates at factor cost. On this basis, public expenditure of all kinds in Britain—excluding expenditure by the nationalised industries—came to 48 per cent of GNP at factor cost in 1974. In the first half of 1975, the figure was almost 53 per cent. The corresponding figure for 1956 was about 38 per cent.

It may be objected that these percentages are still unsatisfactory, for public expenditure includes not only expenditure on goods and services but also social security transfer payments, debt interest, subsidies and so on. These other payments, it is held, raise personal incomes or lower the cost of living and are not therefore a net claim by the state on real resources. It must be admitted that we are dealing here with a mixed bag. It remains true that all these disbursements by the state have to be met by taxation or public borrowing. The truth is there and it is an important one. Even when the state is making transfer payments it is affecting the working of the economy by providing incomes that do not correspond to any current contribution to production. Such transfers, of course, can be justified in principle. In practice the verdict will depend upon the reasons for making them, the scale on which they are being made and the position in which the economy finds itself. To concede as much is very different, however, from pretending that transfers within a nation are of no 'real' economic significance. Public expenditure expressed as a fraction of GNP is admittedly a crude relationship, but it is not without meaning and is convenient and well-established.

Let us, however, try to analyse the figures a little further. The Table relates to expenditure on goods and services only and thus shows the claims made by government in 1974 on real resources. It will be seen that these claims came to 27 per cent of GNP. But we must also allow, on the basis of official assumptions, for the $22\frac{1}{2}$ per cent of personal consumption purchased not from incomes earned in production but from transfers received from the state. Thus officially-financed personal consumption came to nearly 14 per cent of GNP. There was also a substantial item for public expenditure on subsidies and grants of various kinds.

NATIONAL EXPENDITURE IN 1974
(*factor cost*)

	Per cent
Personal consumption	61
Industrial investment (including the nationalised industries)	17
Public authorities' consumption	22
Public investment	5
Exports of goods and services	29
less imports of goods and services	−36
Net unearned income from abroad	2
Gross national product	100

We can now examine a different aspect of public expenditure: its relationship to personal income. Of total personal incomes of almost £75 billion in 1974, about 15 per cent were earned as salaries in central government and local government employment in the production of services that are not marketed. Another 10 per cent was received in the form of social security transfers. Finally a large part of the expenditure by the state on interest went to private persons or to insurance funds and the like operating on their behalf. Thus total personal incomes that did not correspond to the production of marketed goods and services came to not far short of 30 per cent of total personal incomes before tax.

III ECONOMIC CONSEQUENCES OF HIGH EXPENDITURE

What then are the economic consequences of this high level of public expenditure? One of the issues that must be considered is the effect of a high level of public expenditure on inflation.

High government expenditure and inflation

This question was raised by the Expenditure Committee in 1974 and different answers were given by the witnesses.[3] Mr David Worswick was not inclined to accept that there is much connection. He quoted statistics for a number of countries which showed no correlation between the rates of inflation and the relative importance of public expenditure or even between *rates* of inflation and the *rates of growth* of public expenditure. I do not find this altogether surprising when so many other things are not equal. We must admit, however, that although this evidence does not really disprove the case that there is a link between public expenditure and inflation, it shows that there is no simple positive correlation. Any verdict based on this kind of evidence must therefore be 'non-proven'—either way. But we have, here, an interesting field for more detailed comparative research. Why have different rates of inflation been accompanied by differences in the relative importance of public expenditure?

Lord Kahn and Mr Michael Posner were prepared to go further than Mr Worswick. They conceded that a rapid *rate of growth* of public expenditure relatively to the rate of growth of GNP could be inflationary. But they were not prepared to accept that a high *level* of public expenditure was in itself inflationary. This is surely a puzzling view: it is not the destination that matters but only the speed at which it is approached! It would make no difference, therefore, whether public expenditure were only 30 per cent of GNP or over 50 per cent, as it is today. Let us suppose, however, that the percentages were 75 per cent! Or 90 per cent! Can it really be maintained that such percentages would be of no importance provided

---

[3] Ninth Report from the Expenditure Committee: Session 1974.

we did not reach them too quickly? In my view, this is an argument that can easily be demolished by *reductio ad absurdum.*

A relatively large volume of public expenditure may be inflationary in two main ways. First, government may not attempt even from the outset to balance its expenditure by taxation and may finance part of it by borrowing or by the creation of new money. Even if it is financed entirely by long-term borrowing, total monetary expenditure may rise in the short run in so far as the government bonds are purchased by previously idle money. But new money may also be created and has, of course, been created on a vast scale in Britain. It is unnecessary in this context to emphasise the inflationary consequences of the government's net borrowing requirement in recent years or to draw attention to the difficulty, even in 1976, of regaining control. The facts are too painfully familiar.

Suppose, however, that government decided to balance its expenditure fully by taxation. Can we then infer that there will be no inflationary pressure? The answer would appear to be in the affirmative, but it requires closer scrutiny. For we must direct our attention to the strong political and social forces that determine public policy on the money supply. Suppose, then, that government raises public expenditure by a significant amount relatively to national output. Suppose, also, that there is a corresponding rise in taxation imposed with sufficient skill to prevent a deficit from emerging. A higher level of taxation, whether direct or indirect, will reduce the real value of take-home pay and this will produce an incentive to demand higher pay. In short, we have here one of the factors that make for cost-inflation. Unfortunately the monetarists do not want to concede that there is such a phenomenon as cost-inflation because they want to regard changes in the amount of money as the sole factor that can initiate disturbances. But this will not do. Let us, for a moment, consider the sequence of events described by Professor Milton Friedman in a well-known article.[4] An increase in the amount of money leads to a rise in expenditure and a rise in prices. There will, he suggests, be a relative shift in the distribution in favour of profits and at the expense of real wages. This shift may not in practice occur, but let us accept his assumption for the sake of the present argument. Real wages will then fall or, if there is some growth in

---

[4] Milton Friedman, 'The Role of Monetary Policy', *American Economic Review*, March 1968.

total output, real wages may at all events be less than was anticipated when the wage-bargains were made. We are told by the monetarists that there will then be a demand for higher money wages at the existing level of employment. Again let us accept this conclusion. If, however, the erosion of real wages brought about in this way leads to demands for higher money wages, it is surely realistic to say that the erosion of real wages brought about by higher taxation will also lead to demands for higher money wages. It has indeed long been accepted in this country that a rise in indirect taxes may have this effect, but we must also assume that the unions will allow for the impact of higher direct taxes. This point has been stressed by Wilkinson, Turner and Jackson at Cambridge[5] and by Johnston and Timbrell at Manchester.[6] They are surely right.

Let us recall some of the facts about the increasing burden of taxation. A married worker with average earnings paid about a quarter of them in income tax alone in 1975-76 as compared with a tenth in 1960-61. At two-thirds average earnings he was still paying as much as a fifth compared with a twentieth in 1960-61. Is it any wonder that we have had so much pressure for higher pay?

Pressures on government

The monetarists can still object that increased wage demands will not lead to inflation unless the supply of active money is increased. If its supply is not increased and the wage-demands are accepted, or partly accepted, costs will, admittedly, be pushed up and prices will follow unless profit margins can be squeezed; but the penalty will be a lower level of employment and output. It may then be argued that, even if costs and prices rise in this way, such a rise cannot properly be described as inflation for the general level of prices and costs, though jacked up, may stay at something like its new level. Inflation, however, implies successive increases in wages and prices. The weakness of this line of argument is, of course, its neglect of the strong political forces that will come into play. For government is then presented with a harsh dilemma. Should it hold

---

[5] D. Jackson, H. E. Turner and F. Wilkinson, *Do Trade Unions Cause Inflation?*, Occasional Paper 36, Dept. of Applied Economics, University of Cambridge, 1972.

[6] J. Johnston and M. Timbrell, 'Empirical Tests of a Bargaining Theory of Wage Determination', *The Manchester School*, 1973.

expenditure down and thus incur the penalty of higher unemployment and loss of output? Or should it allow total monetary expenditure, public and private, to rise and thus incur the penalty of inflation? It is surely unnecessary to emphasise that government will in practice come under powerful pressure to relax its 'sound money' policy and resort to deficit financing. We are, therefore, forced to conclude that the larger volume of public expenditure and the higher level of taxation can initiate a course of events that will, in the event, be inflationary in the full sense of the term.

Although the monetarists have performed a valuable service by their emphasis on the importance of the money supply, they have marred their case by their too exclusive emphasis on that factor. For this inhibits the investigation of other related matters. Thus we must recognise that most of us are schizophrenic in our approach to public expenditure. We vote cheerfully enough for better roads, hospitals, pensions and so on but we are not prepared to accept the implications for our own real take-home pay. We want higher 'take-home' pay in order to protect or, if possible, to improve our position; and we can bring pressure to bear upon governments to allow these increases in pay to be financed in an inflationary way. For the basic condition of scarcity is not perceived in the same way in forming views about public expenditure as in determining our private expenditure on the market. This, indeed, is the crux. This fact might not have mattered much when public expenditure was less than a tenth of GNP, but it matters enormously when the percentage is in the region of one half.

In short, the belief that government expenditure can be offset by taxation with no inflationary consequences represents an oversimplified interpretation of a complex social situation. It assumes, in particular, that gross incomes are themselves independent of the taxes levied upon them. But this is not so, or is only partly so. For, in practice, higher taxes can lead to higher gross incomes.

High government expenditure and economic growth

I now turn to the possible effect of high public expenditure on economic growth. Mr Robert Bacon and Mr Walter Eltis have presented with great cogency and persuasiveness a case for believing that its effect has been adverse.[7] I shall begin by inviting you to

---

[7] *Sunday Times* for 2, 9, 16 November, 1975, and their essay (No. 1) in this *Readings*.

consider evidence that may suggest doubts. First, let us look much further back in our history. About the beginning of the century government was spending only 10-15 per cent of GNP but the post-war growth of GNP, if slow by international standards, has been fast by our own historical standards. Or let us make an international comparison of the more recent evidence. As with inflation, it does not provide us with any convenient simple correlation. In some other countries such as Germany and France, public expenditure has been nearly as large a proportion of GNP as in Britain but growth has been much faster. Holland has been spending on a rather higher scale but has also done better. The USA has done better with smaller expenditure but not as well as some of the European countries. Japan is the outstanding example that supports what we may call the Bacon-Eltis thesis—with public expenditure at about a fifth of GNP and output rising very rapidly until quite recently.

Admittedly these statistics relate to large aggregates and we should need to break them down in order to make a less superficial analysis. Above all, other things are not equal and this must affect comparisons between countries. If, for other reasons, growth tends to be slow in Britain, then a high and rising burden of public expenditure may be more harmful here than in more buoyant economies. At all events our welfare provisions are not the most generous. Some other countries spend more, even relatively to GNP; but, with faster growth, they do not have to hold back to the same extent the rise in private disposable real incomes. These, however, are complex matters which I cannot pursue further in this paper.

IV RATIONAL ALLOCATION

I return to the problem of making a rational allocation of resources. This is the problem that has occupied the attention of economists for a very long time. How can scarce resources be used most economically?

As I have said, we tend to concentrate attention on allocations made by the market and there are countless textbooks which explain in the most painstaking way to undergraduates that the market may not do this job to complete perfection. There are, however, other central questions of choice and allocation that are very inadequately discussed. Who decides that the state should absorb about 30 per cent of the national output of goods and services and spend in total, including transfers and subsidies, the equivalent of something like two-thirds of GNP? Who decides and by what criteria?

The answer is that no one decides! Public expenditure has simply been allowed to rise year by year, and this is simply the position we have reached so far. The Treasury, for its part, is not really making a choice over a wide range of alternatives. It is hemmed in by the past, and the room for action always seems very restricted. Then there is the familiar problem that a programme adopted at moderate cost in one year may burgeon and grow in subsequent years. This, of course, was the reason for introducing PESC[8] and, in principle, it was right to do so. But PESC has been a disappointment, partly because of too much reliance on so-called survey prices—'funny money', as Sam Brittan calls it. PESC should not be condemned outright for this reason but the procedure needs to be changed. Even so, the spending Ministers may carry their case in Cabinet with little regard to the warnings conveyed by PESC projections. Then there is the question of allocating a given sum of expenditure between public services. We know how difficult it is to devise useful criteria for efficiency. We know how hard it is to ensure that the results of applying such criteria will survive the attack of departmental imperialists within the public service. Faulty allocations may well result. Then there is the further complication that, even given the pattern of preferences, the resources used to achieve these objectives may be used inefficiently. Inefficiency is not, of course, confined to the public service, but private industry is at least subject to the test of the market. It may be a reasonable presumption that there is likely to be more waste in the public service. Inefficiency and waste might be accepted with sadness, but also with resignation, if public expenditure were a small fraction of GNP. It is a different matter when the proportion is so high. It is not only that waste is then larger absolutely but that it is likely to be larger relatively to total public expenditure. For it cannot seriously be doubted that the effectiveness of Treasury control has been considerably reduced by the enormous growth in public expenditure and by the inflation to which it has contributed.

Cutting government expenditure
It is now widely held that we need to reduce the proportion of public expenditure relatively to output. Even the Government agrees.

[8] Public Expenditure Survey Committee.

How is this to be done? The less painful way would be to hold down public expenditure as output starts to rise again when we emerge from the recession. With less unemployment and with rising output per head, we should gradually be able to raise the fraction of output available for private use.[9] It would certainly be exceedingly rash to try to foster recovery by a net increase in public expenditure. If we felt the time had indeed come to reflate, the much wiser course would be to cut taxation. Suppose, however, that this way of reducing the relative amount of public expenditure seems too slow and more drastic action is demanded. It would involve the more painful process of making absolute cuts instead of only reducing proportionately. Admittedly there may be a good deal of scope for reducing waste, including reductions in the number of public employees. In so far as this is true, those who benefit from publicly provided services would not suffer, and the painful process of absolute cuts would be experienced only by people in government employment who were shaken into more effective activity or expelled from the public service.

Savings might be achieved in this way but not, I believe, on a scale sufficient to bring public expenditure down by the required amount. It would then be a question of changing policies, and such changes raise basic questions relating to social welfare and social choice. How should such decisions be made? Could we test public opinion about such changes? I have been told that a senior Treasury official once proposed that people should receive a questionnaire with their tax returns on which they could record their preferences. I don't know whether this story is true, but the idea is an intriguing one. At the very least, we should change our procedure for the handling of public finance. As Sir Alex Cairncross has said, we are the only country in the world where decisions about expenditure are taken before decisions about taxation. The two should obviously be taken together as the Select Committee on Expenditure has now recommended.[10]

---

[9] This is broadly what the Government intends. Even so public expenditure is expected to amount to 53 per cent of GNP in 1979-80. (*Public Expenditure to 1979-80, op. cit.,* p. 8.)

[10] First Report from the Expenditure Committee, session 1975-6, and Minutes of Evidence.

Reform of the welfare state

I have referred to the possibilities of reducing public expenditure relatively to output by allowing output to rise faster than expenditure. I have also referred to the case for doing more than this. The need to do more would be all the greater, of course, if we did not regain even our former modest rate of growth. This is the possibility that has been stressed by Dr Rudolf Klein in a recent publication of the Centre for Studies in Social Policy.[11] 'The escalator has stopped', he says. We may therefore need to think the unthinkable. What this would presumably entail would be a fundamental reform of the welfare state—a reform which would reduce the flow of expenditure but should do so without imposing hardship on those who are really in need, and without blunting our efforts to reduce inequality of opportunity. This would entail a massive slaughter of sacred cows. One wonders when we shall have a Government with sufficient political strength and courage to do so. Shall we *ever* have such a Government? Would there be a better chance of having one if the present electoral system were to be reformed? These are the questions to which we are now led.

Fortunately we need not assume that the escalator—the escalator of growth—has indeed stopped. To this extent the problem will be eased; eased, but not removed. Moreover, the speed of the escalator will depend partly upon our use of scarce resources, and we must scrutinise both critically and constructively the ways in which they are being used. It would be surprising if the verdict did not include a strong recommendation that the claims of the state should be substantially reduced relatively to those of the private sector.

---

[11] *Inflation and Priorities,* edited by Rudolf Klein, 1975.

3. A Model of Inflation and the Government Deficit

JACK WISEMAN

Professor of Applied Economics and Director of the Institute of Social and Economic Research, University of York

THE AUTHOR

JACK WISEMAN was born in 1919 and educated at Nelson Grammar School and the London School of Economics (BSc (Econ.), 1949). Lecturer and Reader at the LSE, 1949-63. He has been Professor of Applied Economics and Director of the Institute of Social and Economic Research, University of York, since 1964. He is Joint Editor of University of York Studies in Economics, and a member of the Editorial Board of the *Journal of Public Finance.*

Professor Wiseman's books include: (with Professor A. T. Peacock) *The Growth of Public Expenditure in the United Kingdom* (1961, 2nd edn. 1967); (with Professor E. H. Phelps Brown) *A Course in Applied Economics* (1964, 2nd edn. 1966); and contributions to *Economica, Economic Journal, Public Finance,* and others.

I have a very long-standing interest in public expenditure problems. Increasingly, I find it very difficult to discuss them save in a context concerned with what is happening in society generally.

The reason for this approach is that I suspect the public expenditure problem cannot be explained in isolation from social phenomena not usually considered by economists. For the most part we are arguing about, and concerned with the symptoms of, a much more fundamental problem and, if we can't deal with that, no proposals are really going to succeed. They may help in the short run but they cannot succeed for long.

Although the public sector deficit can be seen, in the framework of an orthodox Keynesian model, as a *cause* of inflation, there are some strong arguments for seeing it also, in current UK conditions, as a *consequence*.

The dynamics of inflation: towards an economic model?

While there is point in the current concern over the errors that may be encouraged by the government doing its forward planning in real terms, there are underlying real-resource relationships in the economy which are already given too little attention and which may help to explain both the deficit and other current phenomena. None of the separate propositions I want to make are particularly novel. I suspect many of them are not really heavily disputed. I shall try to put them together in some sort of a dynamic process which would suggest to some kinds of economist that I ought to have offered you a formal model. I am not against mathematical modelling of economic processes—it is often very useful and illuminating. But its central deficiency is that the behaviouristic changes that are induced by change itself are extremely difficult to put into this kind of model— the Treasury model, for example. My own view is that experience of inflation in Britain has itself generated behaviour changes that themselves make it much more difficult to produce a reversal. And I have no nicely articulated model to explain this; if it begins to seem worth it I will have to get a bright young man to explain to me what to do.

I am seeing inflation as a time process with two basic characteristics. The first is that a constant rate of inflation over any long period has the same kind of plausibility to me as the notion of a permanently small baby. It really does not happen. We have to expect that, unless something is done to change the situation, the rate of inflation tends to be exponential. And the figures in Britain suggest that certainly has been true here. Long ago, some economists had the notion that ½ per cent per annum inflation was probably a good thing: it oiled the wheels of commerce and so on. But what it also does is to produce 1 per cent inflation next year, and, unless effective counter-inflation policies are used, 2 per cent the next year, and so on. So, first, inflation can't be thought of as a constant or stable social situation. Inflation itself changes the socio-economic relationships and attitudes to policy of people in the community, and may do so in ways impossible or at best very difficult to reverse.

Effects of inflation on government 'balance'

To explain this proposition further I want to postulate an economy in which prices are stable, and which is 'in balance' in the sense that the government's 'take' from the economy is what it wants it to be, and citizens accept (or at least tolerate) that take (which comprises the direct claims over resources removed from citizens by taxes, etc.). I use 'balance' not in the sense that the government has no further plans it would like to implement, but in the broader sense that it has equated the marginal value of such plans with the political loss (in voter support, citizen reaction, or whatever) of attempting to implement them. I term a situation of public expenditure 'balance', then, one in which a government is doing what it thinks it can do politically, and also thinks desirable in the light of its own attitudes.

Now let us allow an externally-induced increase in prices. If the tax system is progressive, the 'take' of government will increase without need for a change in tax rates. We can think of resource-use in the economy being determined by claims (consumption or investment) exercised by:

(a) citizens from their 'own income': i.e. the income left for them to use as they wish after the government has finished with them;

(b) citizens from transfer incomes;

(c) government.

The immediate consequence of the price increase must be to raise the share of claims of the government (c), may lower that of transfers (b), and certainly reduces that of (a), the direct claims of citizens.

Now, if the government was originally 'in balance' in any sense of that term, it would appear that after the price increase it should reduce its own claims, for example by appropriately reducing tax rates. But there are two reasons why it may not do so. First, the 'balance' itself may have been shifted by the inflation. The 'political' equilibrium required a 'marginal' evaluation of benefits from government expansion and of the political disadvantages of raising taxes or borrowing. But now the government 'take' has been increased by inflation: it can choose between the gain from implementing new policies from the newly-available funds, and the loss from not returning the increased 'take' to the citizens. Clearly, the two situations are not identical.

Secondly, if price stability is itself a part of the government's 'balance', orthodox Keynesian policies would require, not the return of the surplus yield generated by taxation, but its sterilisation. Thus, a return to the earlier price level could possibly occur only if, first, the government treats stable prices as an overriding objective; and, secondly, the government policy balance is not changed because

(i) it thinks in terms of relative real share and therefore reproduces the original situation, or

(ii) the citizens in (*a*)—that is the group exercising direct claims on resources—do not notice the deterioration in their position before it is adjusted, and so do not change their behaviour.

And thirdly, the real value of transfer payments (*b*) can be adjusted compatibly with the requisite budget surplus.

Changes in behaviour—and policy

If these conditions are not met—and experience in the UK suggests that they never have been under any government since the Second World War—then the next 'period' (an arbitrary term) is likely to see behaviour changes which create a new policy situation. Let us suppose the government, because its notion of 'balance' changes, predicts that the change in attitude of the residual 'claimants' on community resources (those exercising claims directly) will be slower than any change in its own behaviour. It therefore decides it will extend its own claims over resources and 'accept' (politically) the reduction of the direct claims of citizens. That is, it seeks a new 'balance'.

There are two non-exclusive consequences of this continuing reduction in direct claims. Private investment can be expected to decline, first, because of the reduced size of the direct claims sector, and secondly, because of reduced profitability, particularly in the sectors of private industry which depend on private demand. As a result, real claims on resources from own income continue to fall. 'Lame ducks' appear in the private sector, and the real standards of those who depend upon transfers fall. In time this situation must generate changes in behaviour, either in the government or, if not, in other people. Under (*a*) (the direct claims sector) citizens can react by accepting the reduction in their claims, by working harder or longer, or by taking counter-action. I would suggest that this reaction in Britain has in part taken the form of an evolving and continuous shift from wage, etc. bargaining concerned with relations between the contribution to output of social (trade union, etc.) groups and their incomes, towards bargaining about the relative shares (entitlements) of particular social groups in community output, increasingly without reference to their own contributions to it.

We must here clarify the relation between 'own income' claims on real resources, and transfer payments. They are normally distinguished because transfer payments, it is said, are simply transfers of real claims between one citizen and another. Like all taxonomies, the utility of the distinction depends upon the context in which it is to be used. For our purposes, the important characteristics of the division of real-resource claims from 'own income', from transfer incomes, and from government, are:

(i)   own-income claims are reduced by increases in *either* transfer or government claims; both manifest themselves to the own-income group as a deterioration in their position, which is felt directly—as a diminishing ability to retain or improve standards as they had expected;

(ii) transfer incomes can be protected against reduction (in real terms) only by what might be called 'policy-frustrating' action—that is, by group pressure to maintain the 'relative real share' of the transferees;

(iii) offsetting the decline in direct real-resource claims, there needs to be considered the provision of embodied resources or services in kind (e.g. health services) by the government to the citizens. Thus, the sum of earned income and 'benefits' of this kind has come to be known as the 'social wage'.

It is a characteristic of this process that, while 'public authorities' such as the government or trade union leaders may emphasise the 'social wage' in public discussion, the matter of importance to the worker on the shop floor is the change in his 'direct claim', or 'take-home' pay. Casual observation suggests that this proposition is not unrealistic.

'Real share' bargaining and government expenditure

If this argument is plausible, we can now examine a further stage in this process of change—both of behaviour change and of inflationary development. We are now able, beginning from the arguments made above, to explain the coincidence (compatibility) of phenomena that appear to be incompatible in an orthodox Keynesian model. With continuing inflation, and in the situation we have now introduced, of a possible change in the bargaining habits of the direct claimants—the people who spend the 'residual' income—and with the possibility of groups evolving to maintain 'real' standards in one or other type of transfer payment, we can see the new situation in this way:

If we accept the Keynesian model, the shift of resources to the government could be checked simply by the increasing regressiveness of the tax system, as inflation moves people into higher income brackets. And it has been argued here and there that if we leave everything alone when people do get into a higher bracket, so that the earlier redistribution is no longer occurring, and the 'take' of government is therefore increasing less rapidly, the situation comes under control. But this does not work if the changes in behaviour I have suggested occur in practice. If bargaining shifts towards negotiation about relative shares, and the government has continued to use inflation to extend its own claims, then, first, we can have continued inflation, rising demand for real resources by government, and a (related) relative increase in public sector labour costs. (Notice that the process generates unemployment in the private sector, but can also produce a shift in bargaining attitudes in the public sector.) So now the inflation itself can be generating increases in public sector labour costs. And 'real share' bargaining here can be particularly effective because there is much less possibility of relating earnings changes to changes in public sector output. So that once 'relative share' bargaining begins elsewhere, it is plausible that it may become most effective in the public sector. This does seem to have been happening in the UK.

Secondly, we can simultaneously have increased unemployment, because the process I have been describing reduces profitability and private investment, and because private investment comes out of the 'direct claims' sector which is being squeezed. None of this requires or depends upon any changes in the tax system. The situation will be exacerbated by 'relative share' bargaining in the private sector, and by any shift in the tax system away from personal incomes and towards industry and profits.

Thirdly, we can see here the reasons for the potential emergence of a public sector deficit and an increasing borrowing requirement. Rising transfer payments, rising real labour costs to the public sector, the rising real resource and money costs of expanding government policies, the easier emergence of 'unplanned' policies—that is, the implementation of policies that have not been properly subjected to parliamentary scrutiny (such as the increases in housing subsidies through permissive legislation). In most discussion, the significance of legislation for public expenditures has too little place. Inflation makes this phenomenon extremely important because it enormously raises the cost of implementing agreed policies.

Where have all the millions gone?

Now I turn briefly to examine, within the same general framework, the case of the 'missing' £5,500 million for 1975, which has come to be dubbed the Government's 'unexplained loss'. The breakdown of this £5,500 million is shown in the Table.

		£ million
1.	'Unexplained' deficit	5,500
	Breakdown	
2.	Announced policy changes	1,500
3.	Other volume increases	1,500
4.	Underestimate of relative price effect	1,750
5.	Underestimate of debt interest	750
		£5,500

Item (2) is self-explanatory. Item (3) represents, effectively, 'new' expenditures incurred without need for policy debate. Of the £1,500 million, around £1,000 million can be attributed to government decisions on housing subsidies; the rest remains unexplained. Item (4) indicates a gross under-calculation of the relative price effect, arguably because of the inflation-induced change in the bargaining environment already explained. Item (5) is more difficult to explain. Over the relevant period, inflation rates were higher than the general level of interest rates: we would therefore expect a rise in current money interest payments, but not in the size of real transfers from this source.

'Announced policy changes' are expenditure obligations of government implied by legislation already passed through Parliament. The problems arise from the growing volume of 'permissive' legislation, which makes it difficult to forecast increasing spending under this head with any accuracy. 'Other volume increases', on the other hand, is civil service jargon for *unannounced* changes in policy. This is government 'policy expenditure' that has not been explicitly debated or subjected to legislative discussion anywhere. The simplest illustration is that £1,000 million of the £1,500 million of 'Other volume increases' has been attributed to increases in housing subsidies which are not subjected to specific public scrutiny. It is not clear where the remaining deficit of £500 million should be allocated.

When we examine the underestimation of the relative price effect, it should be noted that the discrepancy is the *outcome*, on our interpretation, of the inflationary process itself: it does not result simply from differing labour intensities in the public and private sectors giving different relations between labour and output through time. This change is allowed for. What is being underestimated is the effect of inflation itself on such elements as the wage-bargaining process.

Efficacy of 'control systems'

My conclusions must be tentative since my model is itself tentative. The general proposition I would make is that all kinds of 'control systems' are likely to be of limited utility unless any 'breathing space' they provide is used to break down the dynamic process I have described. This in turn requires that people's expectations about the future course of prices, etc., must be changed.

'Cash ceilings'—another fad?

The current vogue for 'cash ceilings' may therefore be of only limited relevance. The Dutch used a not dissimilar, but arguably more sophisticated, system some years ago, called the 'structural budget margin'. Essentially, it used budgetary procedure to throw up the 'margin' available for 're-allocation' between new public policies and increased 'direct claims' by citizens through tax reductions. The reason for the breakdown of this system is also the weakness of the 'cash limits' approach. 'Cash limits' are valuable in throwing up for scrutiny the practical implications of incremental changes in the budget 'balance'. But included in the 'balance' (and hence the decision) are inevitably elements of judgement about reactions. The decision about the *ceilings* is, inevitably, a decision about *policy*. If a cash ceiling is required by a government to be implemented, then, at least implicitly, the government has accepted responsibility for the (policy) implications of that requirement. (Refusal to provide further subsidy funds, i.e. above the previously agreed total, for a nationalised industry faced with a wage bid is effectively an expression of willingness to accept the related consequences of a possible strike.)

This reasoning, incidentally, seems to throw light on the relative position of the monetarists and other economists. In the last analysis monetarists would require the subsidisation/borrowing of nationalised industries to be restricted. This implies, for example, that they would have to be prepared to accept and sit out a miners' strike rather than increase the subsidy to coal. What remains generally unexplained is how the social conflicts generated by the imposition of restrictive cash ceilings will be resolved.

The root cause . . .

The root cause of the problem lies in government and in government policies, and the only way in practice to handle it ultimately is to find ways to make the government regard the resources over which it automatically gets control through inflation as not properly belonging to government, and somehow to relate policy to that simple truth. A part of this might be done by better flow of information. But certainly some of it has to be done by a very serious change of heart, and that on the part of more than one Department and political party. The Labour Party is not the only one that says: 'Poor pensioners, they must be protected automatically against things like inflation'. Conservatives have said that pensions should be reviewed every six months. And in saying that they show their humanity. But the need to exercise humanity arises out of the process I have analysed. People like pensioners are suffering in the first place because government is not willing to make uncomfortable decisions that would remove the necessity for suffering, and the cure adopted for the suffering generates further inflation.

Finally, let me repeat my general theme. Inflation itelf must be expected to change economic behaviour, and there are plausible hypotheses about dynamic (ongoing) changes of this kind which would appear to explain many of the current intellectual anomalies (notably the continued persistence of inflation and unemployment). The growth of public expenditure is a predictable outcome of the process described. It follows that effective long-term control of expenditures must depend upon the checking or reversal of the present dynamics of inflation.

PART II
The Parliamentarians

4. Instruments and Machinery for Control

DAVID HOWELL

THE AUTHOR

DAVID HOWELL was born in 1936 and educated at Eton and King's College, Cambridge (B.A. 1st Class Honours, 1959). He has been Conservative MP for Guildford since 1966. He was Minister of State, N. Ireland Office, 1972-74, and at the Dept. of Energy, 1974. He has written several books including *The Conversative Opportunity* (1965). He is married with two children.

There are no difficulties at all in listing the reasons why the public expenditure issue causes such widespread concern. Public expenditure is unhealthily high as a proportion of Gross Domestic Product; much too much power is accruing to the state authorities; the financing of public expenditure has deeply serious implications for monetary policy and a direct bearing on inflation; the tax system is hopelessly overloaded, with all its faults and weaknesses magnified; bureaucracy is spreading, performance worsening, precious technical manpower has been sucked away from productive industry.

The difficulty about public expenditure begins with the next stage —where one has to define precisely what is wrong, how to put it right, what parts of the machinery must be changed, what new instruments are needed, how they should be used and how their use should be timed. Rhetoric comes easily. The remedies require a diamond-edged precision of thought, analysis and action of a kind far less easily available.

Five essential requirements

First, then, what precisely are the requirements on which we have to focus? They can be found from within the general statements with which I began, but they need refinement. For clarity I put them here under five headings.

(a) *Changing policies*

Policy determines expenditure, but how do policy changes become translated into reduced public spending? How are they fed into the onward rolling stream of public expenditure commitments? At what point do the politicians put in their oar? Should policy changes be centrally determined? or should Ministers stick to a more general target—the percentage of public expenditure in GDP—and leave the whole administrative machine, centrally and locally, to throw up policy changes and to sift and shake out activities as best it can within the overall constraints placed upon it?

(b) *The economic, fiscal and monetary contexts*

How important is it to assess public expenditure totals in a 'demand' context, how important in terms of impact on taxation levels, and how important in a monetary context? At what point in the annual cycle are these assessments best made? How are the conclusions for policy reached? And how are they used and in what form must they be presented to the strategic decision-makers so as to have a real impact on agreed public expenditure levels?

(c) *Making cuts stick: the instruments*
Once the will to cut spending is there, how is it translated into action? By the Ministers adhering doggedly to predetermined cash limits or by challenging specific programmes? What are the difficulties for central departments of central government (Treasury, Civil Service Department, Cabinet Office), and Ministers working through these departments when it comes to eliminating functions and activities inside spending departments? Can functions in practice be cut without challenging major policies? Or should the Treasury stick to money and leave departments to work out their own detailed cuts?

(d) *Cutting down bureaucracy in government*
It is said that millions can be saved by reducing bureaucracy and increasing efficiency in central and local government. This is correct. But how and by whom? Is it imagined that any central body in government would ever have the manpower, the knowledge or even the authority to sift through innumerable departments and divisions of public authority? Or can it be done by vastly more delegation of responsibility or by creating that sense of personal commitment to cutting costs and the increased efficiency of operations which good management should engender? If so, how?

(e) *Manpower in public employment*
Cut the numbers, some say, and all else will follow. But can numbers be cut unless functions are cut, or policies dropped? And if present activities can be done with less people, who is to adjudicate on how many? The Civil Service Department (CSD) with its Management Services Divisions? Or the spending department, which knows more about its activity than the CSD ever will and whose officials may regard outside suggestions for doing things differently as implied criticism of their past performance? Or the civil service unions, with their very strong interest in keeping the numbers up and their power to resist changes and reductions?

I do not myself believe that these questions are unanswerable or the matters they raise insuperable, although there are many who do, and many more who don't care very much. But my strong plea is that it is from these detailed questions rather than from platform generalities that the work must begin, otherwise nothing very much will happen.

(a) Changing policies to restrain expenditure

When a new government comes into office it has changes in policy it wants to introduce. In 1970, most of the Conservative Party's policies, although admittedly not all, were devised with the desire to restrain public spending firmly in mind. This purpose of course will be even more essential next time. Even to produce policies in Opposition which will reduce rather than increase public spending is not at all easy. It is all too easy to succumb to the temptation to blur the problem by saying 'this is what we will do', then adding in small print 'when the economic situation allows', and thus feel one's duty in the matter of cutting public spending has been done.

Let us say a Government reaches office with policy changes in mind to cut spending. Is this enough? The answer is no. There is first the task of feeding the policy changes into the public expenditure cycle, and this can be vastly time-consuming. Review committees and committees of officials will spring into existence to examine how the future can be dovetailed on to the past without dislocation. By the time every argument has been heard, the public expenditure processes for Year One will be too far down the line. From this I draw Lesson No. 1—policy changes must be formulated and fed into the decision-making processes at the very earliest stage. Trying to cut public spending by changing policy—or by feverishly trimming the edges of policy—halfway through the annual cycle, or when the figures have been collected by the Treasury and have gone to the Cabinet, is like trying to stop a tank with a bale of straw. It is far, far too late.

The business of policy formulation and of reaching policy decisions and then inserting them into the administrative machine is in itself a vast area full of problems and difficulties, some of which we Conservatives tried to tackle in the early 1970's with our measures to strengthen the policy-making machinery at the heart of government.

But even if one succeeds, that is far from sufficient. Policy changes, especially those which might require cuts in public spending, have a habit of melting away or being indefinitely postponed once they reach departments, unless there exists in the Cabinet not merely a vague hope that expenditure ought to be cut but a collective determination that it shall be held within a specific ceiling as a matter of long-term strategic policy.

In other words, brave decisions taken to change policy are part of the story. But they are impotent by themselves unless Cabinet Ministers, thinking as Cabinet Ministers and not as departmental chiefs, are at the same time collectively engaged in the task of reducing, or limiting the growth of, public spending in line with some specific long-term measurement which reflects their values and principles about the way society should be divided between individual and collective activities.

(b) The demand, fiscal and monetary contexts

But we are not there yet. Assume a marvellous range of policy changes, all of which would lead to lower public spending. Assume a marvellous collective determination in the incoming Cabinet to keep public expenditure at, say, 45 per cent of GDP. Assume that the policy changes are fed in so skilfully and are constructed so well that the administrative system digests them and the departments take them aboard. Assume even that Ministers do not immediately return to their departments and connive in resisting what they have collectively agreed at Downing Street a few hours or days before.

All that is still not enough. To see what more is needed we must turn to the 'demand' and monetary restraints which ought to operate on public spending and the way in which they too must be introduced into the decision-making process. Here, we must scrutinise more closely the cycle of public expenditure determination.

At a certain point in the year, say about April/May, but it can be earlier, the Treasury seeks bids from departments about their spending for the coming year. These are then collated by the Treasury and presented to Treasury Ministers for assessment of the total figure. But assessment in the light of what? We can be sure that the assessment in the British Treasury will be in the light of demand on resources. This is a side of Treasury work which has been very well developed. It will probably be suggested to Ministers that the total in Year One (and for the sake of realism I shall ignore those wonderful years in which to cut expenditure, Two, Three, Four and Five!) is either too large in relation to forecasts of total demand on resources or too small, or, as far as the Treasury can judge, about right. In the first case bilateral arguments with department officials will have to begin to see how much can be sliced off. In the last case, Treasury Ministers may be told that a little more can always be added during the year (there is never a shortage of candidates for extra spending). Alternatively, Ministers will be reminded that higher expenditure will have to be balanced by tax increases to satisfy the total demand constraints. Or that a combination of both expenditure cuts and higher taxation may be required. If the Treasury thinks the total looks about right, the next stage is to tidy up the ends with departments and prepare for the Cabinet's first examination of the global figures.

So much for the 'demand' and fiscal judgements that have to be made. What about the monetary aspect? Here we are in a much murkier area—where some of the most serious errors of judgement have been allowed to develop and fester. Without raking over too many embers, let me put it like this. I regard it as of the first importance that the public expenditure totals for the coming Year One should be properly assessed in the light of their impact on the borrowing requirement, the money supply, the structure of interest rates, the gilt-edged market, the structure of savings and the balance of payments. Fiscal policy is also of course relevant in this context.

This assessment should be made by the Treasury Ministers and then by the Cabinet as a whole in full knowledge of the facts and estimated consequences by the monetary authorities. It is not a matter that can be settled privately between the Chancellor and the Governor of the Bank of England, or worse still between the Treasury and senior officials of the Bank of England. On the contrary, it is a central issue of public policy in the handling of which the minds of all senior members of the Government—indeed ideally all members of the Government and the appropriate committees of Parliament— should be heavily engaged. To say that the monetary context does not matter is to say that money does not matter. I hope—although I am not sure—that we have now all learned in Whitehall and Westminster where that kind of thinking leads. Whether this has been the missing dimension in the past I do not know. But I do know it is the critical dimension now.

To sum up so far, I see the monetary assessment of public expenditure totals, the 'demand' assessment, the fiscal assessment and the broad political judgement about the percentage of GDP as being four legs of a chair. If one is missing the strategy of public expenditure restraint will not stand up. Taken together the four can provide the support required for the Cabinet's collective determination to hold public expenditure at specific levels. Ministers must have before them the knowledge that to exceed the specific levels will mean not only that the percentage is getting too high as a proportion of GDP, or that there will be additional problems for the Revenue and the probability of tax increases or no tax cuts—these consequences are serious enough—but also that to exceed the limits will have direct and disastrous implications for monetary policy, for interest rates and for inflation. And to them they can add the 'thought for today' that high interest rates and high inflation can be more disastrous for investment and jobs than any short-term effects caused by the restraint of public expenditure.

(c) The instruments of expenditure control

Equipped in this way—and only when they are equipped in this way—Ministers will be in a position to dig in. This brings us to the third aspect of the struggle—the question of devising the right instruments—in particular the use of cash limits as the key instrument for putting the Cabinet's will into effect.

When the Conservative Party came into power in 1970 we set much store by the need not merely to change policies (on which we had a number of ideas, some worked out, some not so well worked out), but to challenge, question, and if possible cut a considerable range of functions and activities in Whitehall.

We were much less worried at that stage about local government, and, I fear, knew much less about what was going on. Concern about local government spending tended to be met with the argument that 'the whole thing' was going to be reorganised anyway and we should not, as Conservatives, interfere too much in the detail of local government activities. Our main contribution in this area was to encourage major local authorities to use better programme and policy analysis before embarking on projects. To judge from today's situation in local government we should have pressed even harder than we did.

We also put heavy emphasis, I think rightly, on the need to control and monitor continuing programmes and to question outputs and objectives systematically and regularly. To this end we were anxious to bring to Whitehall some, if not all, of the thinking lying behind the Programming, Planning Budgeting System (PPBS) and other systems then being tried out in several governments around the world, with varying degrees of success.

I do not think our interest in questioning programmes and cutting functions was misplaced, but it was obviously not enough. I must explain why. It is a question of back-up and political support. A Treasury or CSD view that a certain departmental function should cease is bound to be unpopular. If the usual delaying devices fail there will be appeals to the departmental Minister and he in turn will be urged by officials to take the issue to his colleagues. But if it is common knowledge that Ministers collectively are sticking to cash limits firmly, the resistance will stop there. The case for cutting will be ruefully conceded. By contrast, if spending is the order of the day the appeal will always be made, the political difficulties of the proposed cut magnified to the maximum, and the 'cutting' lobby will lose nearly every battle. In other words, without a genuine pattern of cash limits imposed on departments and supported at the highest political level, the function-cutting approach loses its edge. In the end, everyone knows, Ministers will prefer the quiet life. The would-be zealots for economy can be safely outflanked.

The advent of 'cash limits'

The term 'cash limits' is being thrown around nowadays to mean many things. In the broader sense I suppose it means that both the Treasury and departments should move away from the habit of happily discounting rising wages and prices in their programmes and thinking only in terms of real resources. In other words it should be taken on board in central and local government that money matters.

Within this general approach, a number of techniques can be developed. Some open-ended expenditures—unemployment benefit, for instance—are obviously very difficult candidates for cash limits. Elsewhere, the introduction of cash limits really means changing the policy—which may hitherto have laid down that certain benefits should always be paid on certain criteria at certain given rates. And some kind of conditions may have to be attached to the cash limits, to allow some specified degree of manoeuvre and flexibility, if they are to be realistic. Effective monitoring is also essential.

But whether refined or in crude form, the cash limits approach is the essential and hitherto missing tool in the hands of the Treasury when dealing with departments. This is certainly not to say that all ideas for questioning programmes and challenging functions from the centre should be discarded. This kind of prodding and pushing from the Treasury and the CSD is undoubtedly valuable. But there are severe limits to what it can achieve on its own without the cash limits 'long stop'.

There are two further reasons for caution in the 'detailed' approach to spending cuts. First, if there is too much harassing from the centre on specifics, life in the Department for the departmental Ministers becomes impossible. This is the way to the absurdly over-detailed control of expenditure which the Treasury mistakenly practised in the past and which leads to paralysis and demoralisation (although not necessarily to less spending). If the Treasury is to go in for budgetary questioning of a detailed and analytical kind, it must have an extremely sensitive touch.

PAR

The system of Programme Analysis and Review (PAR), which was designed to give central departments and Ministers collectively a fundamental view of major programmes at regular intervals, provides the right framework for this kind of work. PAR did not get off to a very good start, but it remains an important part of the questioning and control processes for a healthy bureaucracy.

The second reason why the specific approach has limited effect is, I am afraid, a little more cynical. It is simply that the Treasury and other central departments can never know as much in as much detail as the spending departments about what they are doing. This means that every proposal from the centre for an activity to be cut can be met with the counter-proposal that it be reviewed, or that outside management consultants be brought in, or that it is already being covered by some other review, or that a working party be set up on which, of course, the Treasury or the CSD are invited to have representatives.

It does not take a genius to see that in this way one soon runs out of manpower. Whole armies of systems analysts and dedicated cost-cutters can be swallowed up in interminable reviews and studies. And at the end of it—which may be several years on—the possible gains may be rather slight.

This is not always the case. Valuable changes and excellent streamlining can certainly be achieved. So I do not want to decry this side of the campaign aginst rising public spending. But, I repeat, it is not enough by itself. The cash limits approach is the other indispensable element, and that in turn depends upon the inflexible will of senior Cabinet Ministers acting together. And this in turn rests, or so I have suggested, on the four fundamental and central policy judgements which it is the duty of the Cabinet to reach, and to adhere to constantly.

(d) The war on bureaucratic inefficiency

I will now expand a little on one further aspect of control of government spending, and that is the campaign for more efficiency. Call it 'anti-bureaucratisation' or even 'de-departmentalisation', since it is often the departmental embrace which gives a well-run government programme its coating of red-tape and complexity and from which it only needs to be disengaged to be run efficiently again.

From the time of the Fulton Report onwards, immense efforts have been made in Whitehall to increase operational efficiency and instal sensible management structures. These efforts have certainly borne fruit, although in the absence of the right policy climate and the right machinery in the areas I have discussed the going has been very hard indeed.

In 1970 the incoming Government worked well with the Civil Service and with departments in taking these matters further. We also argued, I think rightly, that the general questioning approach we wished to introduce in our search for economies and our desire to cut functions would itself create a crisper atmosphere and induce departmental officials to rethink what they were doing and do it better.

The key, of course, is delegation. Whitehall departments are over-centralised and they have a centralising influence on everything they touch. Our aim therefore was to push out from the centre as much as we could, either into departmental agencies or into separate and hived-off bodies. All this effort raised and still raises serious problems of financial control and public accountability. If departmental civil servants are going to be called to account for the spending activities of an agency, their natural inclination is to keep as much control of spending decisions in it as they can. Against this, efficient management rightly demands a substantial degree of budgetary freedom— indeed an element of competition, if it can be arranged. I do not think these objects are irreconcilable, but they have to be worked out patiently and skilfully in every case.

(e) The growing army of government employees

Finally, manpower. The Conservatives did in fact operate between 1970 and 1974 a sort of manpower limit on the central government Civil Service akin to the cash limits technique. It was not a complete failure but it did not work very well for the simple reason that other things were considered more important—even if these things involved more civil servants, sometimes in very great numbers.

The lessons to be drawn are similar to those I raised in discussing cash limits. If the collective will of senior Ministers is strong enough, and if it is rooted in a deep understanding of the overriding political importance of holding the limit, and of the serious consequences of exceeding the limit, it will be held. If there is no collective will, or if minds are on other things, the task is difficult, if not hopeless. It can certainly be said that to enforce manpower ceilings without cash limits, backed up by pressure to change policies and eliminate functions, is an impossible task. But, if all these other pressures are operating effectively, manpower controls undoubtedly have an important part to play.

*   *   *   *   *

In summing up, let me put what I have spelt out in this shorthand form. The collective and political will to cut spending must exist; it cannot be conjured out of thin air. It must be founded not only upon well-formulated policy changes but on thorough assessments and crystal-clear presentation of the full implications, social, economic and monetary, of the public expenditure totals put before Ministers for approval. Moreover, collective political will cannot be sustained or translated into action without the proper machinery working in the proper phasing; 'will' and machinery go together. If that part of the operation is working, the power is there to make the instruments of control operate. By these I mean first, cash limits, supported secondly by function-cutting, sustained promotion of increased efficiency and manpower controls.

When and if all these policies work in the same direction, there are grounds for believing that public expenditure will again be under some kind of control and that bureaucracy, while never cured (one cannot after all deny a bureaucracy the right to be bureaucratic), will at least be restrained.

And if it still all looks too easy, behind the simple phrases like 'collective will' lie far far deeper considerations. Holding a Cabinet full of powerful political figures and ambitious spending Ministers together is plainly a difficult enough task. Creating a sense of common endeavour in which each of them will think first as a Cabinet Minister, and only second as a departmental head, requires even greater feats of leadership and command of parliamentary support. That it can be done, indeed that it will be done, I am confident. But to explain the reasons for my confidence would open up still wider issues.

5.   A Social-Democratic View

DAVID MARQUAND

THE AUTHOR

DAVID MARQUAND was born in 1934 and educated at Emanuel School, Magdalen College and St. Anthony's College, Oxford (1st Class Honours in Modern History, 1957). He has been a lecturer (University of Sussex, 1964-66) and leader-writer (*Guardian*, 1959-62). Labour MP for Ashfield since 1966. He was a member of the Select Committee on Estimates, 1966-68. He is the son of Rt. Hon. Hilary Marquand, PC, is married and has two children.

For most of their history, the Labour Party in general, and its social-democratic wing in particular, have supported and even advocated high levels of public expenditure almost on principle. In part, no doubt, this is merely because the measures needed to alleviate the poverty and distress which the Labour Party came into existence to combat have almost always entailed increases in public expenditure in practice. But there are deeper reasons as well, and any worthwhile attempt to define a social-democratic approach to the current debate about public expenditure must begin by examining them.

In the first place, the Labour Party has always stood for more social and economic equality. In the days when public-expenditure programmes mainly benefited the poor, while the taxes to pay for them were levied mainly on the better off, the net effect was redistributive. As a result, it came to be assumed that public spending was *ipso facto* egalitarian and, as such, *ipso facto* socialist. Secondly, it is important to remember that socialism grew up in reaction to the excesses of the individualistic capitalism of the early ninteenth century. From the first, one of its most important elements was a belief in the desirability of communal action as such—a belief that sprang partly from a revulsion against the hardship and suffering that excessive individualism brought with it, and partly from a revulsion against the curiously bloodless and inhumane social theories which justified that hardship and suffering. Thus, socialists tended to assume that publicly-provided goods were inherently better—more beneficial to their recipients, and more productive of social welfare—than were privately-provided goods.

Is public expenditure a 'good thing'?

Both these assumptions made excellent sense in the days when they first grew up. As recently as ten years ago, when I was first elected to the House of Commons, they still provided a reasonably good guide to public policy. But although much of the current anxiety about high levels of public expenditure seems to me misplaced, and although many of the proposals made for reducing the level of public expenditure seem to me foolish and dangerous, there can be no doubt that the traditional social-democratic assumption that public expenditure is, of its very nature, 'a good thing' now needs to be re-examined.

For it has become clear during the last ten years that although our constituents welcome, and even demand, high levels of public expenditure in their capacities as voters, they rebel against the consequences of high levels of public expenditure in their capacities as taxpayers and, more damagingly, in their capacities as trade unionists. If public expenditure grows more quickly than the gross national product, one of two things has to happen. Either the increase in expenditure will be financed by adding to the borrowing requirement, with the inflationary consequences we know so well. Or it will be financed by increases in taxation, which bear, increasingly heavily, not only on the better off, but on the average wage-earner as well. And although the average wage-earner may want—may even have vociferously demanded—the goods on which public money has been spent, he is apt to be less enthusiastic about paying for them. When the tax collector presents the bill, the wage-earner responds by putting in for higher wage increases so as to restore his disposable income to its old level. And that, I suspect, has been an even more important cause of the inflation of the last few years than was the expansion in the money supply of the early 1970s. The often-canvassed notion that high levels of public expenditure are in some way inimical to rapid economic growth seems to me wildly over-simplified at best, and dangerously misleading at worst. That there is a causal connection between very rapid increases in the proportion of GDP absorbed by public expenditure, on the one hand, and increases both in cost and in demand inflation, on the other, seems to me beyond dispute.

Secondly, it has become clear during the last ten years that the pattern of public expenditure is determined, not by conscious choice on the part of the society whose needs that expenditure is supposed to satisfy, and not even by the conscious choice of the elected representatives of that society, but by a haphazard combination of *ad hoc* political pressure, departmental log-rolling and bureaucratic inertia. In that combination, moreover, bureaucratic inertia is clearly by far the most important element. The motto of the spending department is the First World War refrain: 'We're here because we're here because we're here'; and where we are today determines where we will be tomorrow. The early socialists were right when they pointed out that classical economic theory broke down because the economy is made up of human beings and not of Benthamite calculating machines. Modern social democrats should remember that exactly the same is true of the public sector. The civil servants and local government officials who decide how public money is spent in detail in the real world, and whose decisions produce the great aggregates debated around the Cabinet table and published in the annual expenditure White Papers, are not bloodless automata. They have interests to pursue, jobs to protect, empires to build. They want what is best for the society they serve: there can be no question about that. But they are almost bound to believe that they can serve society best by continuing to do the jobs they already do in the way that they already do them. Often, they are right. But, right or wrong, they constitute an independent interest group of formidable weight, and no discussion of the role of public expenditure in a complex modern society will get very far unless they are seen as such.[1]

Middle-class pressure or the 'affluent society'?

Thirdly, it is becoming increasingly clear that public expenditure is not *ipso facto* egalitarian in the way that most social democrats used to assume it was bound to be. Recently, Tony Crosland, who could perhaps be described as the high priest of British social democracy, and who certainly used to be the high priest of public expenditure, confessed in a Fabian pamphlet:

> 'We under-estimated the capacity of the middle classes to appropriate more than their fair share of public expenditure. They demand more resources for the schools in their areas; they complain vociferously if they have to wait for their operations; they demand that the state intervene to subsidise the prices of the rail tickets from their commuter homes to their work. Too often these pressures have been successful, and in consequence the distribution of public spending has been tilted away from the areas of greatest need to those which generate the loudest demands'.

Crosland's formulation, I must admit, seems to me over-simplified. He seems to be suggesting that pressure from middle-class areas is the sole reason for the 'tilting' in public expenditure of which he

---

[1] [*The Economics of Politics* is the title of a forthcoming Hobart Paper by Professor Gordon Tullock of Virginia State University and Dr. Morris Perlman of the London School of Economics.—Ed.]

complains. I suspect that it is only one reason, and that a much more fundamental—and, for a socialist, a much more disquieting—reason is that we now live in an affluent society in which, not only a middle-class minority, but most weekly wage-earners as well, have more to lose than to gain from egalitarian public-expenditure decisions. To take only the most flagrant example, it is not just the middle class which clamours for better roads. Affluent workers do so too: and there is no evidence that either group loses much sleep over the plight of the poor minority whose taxes help to pay for the roads but who cannot afford cars to drive on them. But even if Mr Crosland is wrong about the cause, he is undoubtedly right about the consequence. The old notion that public expenditure necessarily redistributes income from the better off to the worse off is simply not true. Some forms of public expenditure do: others don't. Some may even redistribute it from the worse off to the better off.

Fourthly, it is, to put it mildly, doubtful whether the huge increases which have taken place in public expenditure over the past ten years have produced commensurate improvements in the services concerned. Most of us would probably agree that the road network is, in 1976, significantly better than it was in 1966. The improvement has been purchased at vast expense, and it is arguable that the damage it has done to the quality of life in urban areas outweighs the benefits it has brought to the economy. All the same, it is a real improvement. It would be hard to argue that there has been as great an improvement in the health service, the postal service, the crime-prevention service or (in spite of smaller classes) in the education service. I do not suggest for one moment that the public sector is alone in failing to get value for the money it spends. On the contrary, waste and inefficiency are rampant in the private sector too; and no one who has watched the abysmal performance of Britain's privately-owned industries over the past ten years can possibly hold them up as models for the public sector. But that is not the point. The point is that, in the past, socialists used to assume that the public sector would perform *better* than the private sector, and that it demonstrably has not.

The traditional approach and present-day reality

For all these reasons, it seems to me clear that the social democratic wing of the Labour Party, at any rate, has a clear obligation to re-examine its traditional, rather *simpliste* approach to public

70

expenditure, and see whether it can develop a more sophisticated conception, fitting the realities of present-day society. This is clearly a major exercise. Here I can only indicate in very general terms what seems to me to be the right approach.

The first and most obvious point is that we need much more sophisticated criteria for determining our public-expenditure priorities and for determining the proper balance between public expenditure and private consumption. The suggestion that public expenditure should be 'reined back', or even 'cut back', to some arbitrarily-determined proportion of GDP is as *simpliste* as the suggestion that public expenditure is always and of its very nature desirable. Public expenditure is not all of a piece. Transfer payments are different from expenditure on goods and services—an obvious point, but one which seems to have escaped many of the more hysterical contributors to the current debate. They are different, moreover, not simply from an economic point of view but from a political point of view and even, I believe, from a moral and philosophical point of view. If citizen A gives up some of his income, and therefore some of his freedom of choice, in order to increase the income, and therefore the freedom of choice, of citizen B, the whole transaction raises quite different questions from those raised when citizens A and B both hand over part of their incomes to the state, which then spends the money in their names.

There are wide differences even within that part of public expenditure that goes on goods and services. Some goods—law and order, military security—can be provided only by the public sector. Others —parks in city centres, nuclear power, facilities for advanced medical research—could in theory be provided by the private sector, but in practice won't be, either because the costs are too high or because the benefits are too diffuse. In some cases—education and medical care are perhaps the best examples—the decision as to whether they should be provided privately or publicly depends on a complex series of value-judgements about the nature of the good society and is almost bound to be fiercely controversial. In other cases—the products of the Rolls-Royce plant at Hucknell in my constituency spring irresistibly to mind—goods formerly provided by the private sector are now provided by the public sector, not because anyone particularly wanted to make the change, but because the Government of the day had no practical alternative.

Given these distinctions—and it would not be difficult to make others, equally valid—it is clearly absurd to call, in general terms, for a halt to increases in public expenditure, and then to sit back, satisfied that one has done one's bit for economic realism. Indeed, it is not only absurd: it is also dangerous. Some forms of public expenditure need, not just to be held static, but to be cut back, notably the road programme. Others—expenditure on industrial training is my own favourite example, but it is not the only one— require rapid expansion, even in the coldest of cold climates. But the existing pattern of expenditure is what it is because of the enormous weight of the political and other pressures which have produced it. Those pressures will be felt at least as strongly when cuts are made as they were when increases took place. Thus, to call generally for cuts in planned spending programmes without saying where the knife should fall is almost certainly to ensure that it will fall in the wrong place. If we are to make sure that it falls in the right place, we must have the right priorities. And before we can decide our priorities we must know what criteria to use.

Criteria for cuts: equality and choice

What are the right criteria for a social democrat? As stated above, one of the central pillars of social democracy is a belief in equality —a belief that all men and women should have, so far as possible, an equal chance to develop their potentialities to the full, an equally civilised environment and equal access to the resources needed for self-fulfilment. There is also a second pillar, however, which has sometimes been neglected. This is a belief in liberty, in freedom of choice. For social democracy is a child of nineteenth-century liberalism—a rebellious and awkward child, perhaps, but still part of the family.

The early socialists differed furiously with their liberal contemporaries about the practical implications of their common liberal philosophy. Nineteenth-century liberals believed that that philosophy could be realised best if state activity were kept down to the minimum. Socialists correctly pointed out that if the activities of the state were kept down to the minimum, the strong would flourish while the weak went to the wall. But although socialists fought for a strong, interventionist state, so as to redress the balance of the market-place in favour of the poor and the weak, they did so in the name of the same liberal principles which the people against whom they fought also upheld. I do not suggest that these principles provide a precise formula, which will tell us how to take all our public-expenditure decisions in future. I do suggest that they provide a better guide to policy than the feckless assumption that all public expenditure is equally good—or than the panic belief that all public expenditure is equally bad.

Controlling the juggernaut

At the moment, however, the machinery to translate these—or, indeed, any other—principles into practice simply does not exist. Tony Crosland's judgement that public expenditure has been 'tilted' in what he and I would both consider to be the wrong direction was an impressionistic one. Though I am sure he is right, I have no way of knowing precisely *how far* he is right about each particular spending programme. Some spending departments have a fairly precise idea of who gets what out of at least some of the money they spend: supplementary benefits are an obvious case in point. Others probably have at any rate a rough-and-ready idea. Others, I strongly suspect, have no idea whatever. The first essential of a social democratic policy for public expenditure is therefore to establish, in detail, exactly which income groups benefit from the various expenditure programmes at present and to what extent. The techniques needed to do this will obviously have to vary a good deal from one spending programme to another, and in some cases—defence expenditure, for example, or law enforcement—some rather arbitrary assumptions will have to be made. But although total enlightenment is impossible, we can get a good deal nearer it than we are now.

The second essential, it seems to me, is a thorough overhaul of the existing decision-making process. For the existing process is not only haphazard in its results; it is also scandalously undemocratic. I doubt very much if it is possible to reform the distribution of public expenditure without reforming the machinery by which it is distributed. Even if it were, reforms in the machinery would still be necessary for their own sake. A small step was taken in the right direction a few years ago when the Select Committee on Procedure, on which David Howell and I both served, successfully recommended the publication of annual public expenditure white papers, the holding of annual public expenditure debates and the establishment of a functionally-organised Select Committee on Expenditure. But the step was pathetically small in relation to the need, and it now requires to be followed by a whole series of much bigger steps.

The expenditure committee should be expanded, so as to cover each spending department with a permanent parliamentary committee. Each committee would then go through 'its' department's forward estimates, taking evidence from the minister and from the officials in charge of each of the main sub-programmes. The minister would be required to justify his proposals to the committee, in the way that Treasury ministers now have to justify proposed tax changes to the Standing Committee on the finance bill, and the committee would either accept or reject them. It would then report accordingly to the House, which would then endorse or fail to endorse its report.

A structure of that kind would obviously involve a revolutionary change in the relationship between the executive and the legislature, and equally revolutionary changes in the functioning of the House of Commons and perhaps also in the relationship between the political parties. It would be fiercely resisted by traditionalists on both sides of the Chamber, by the front benches of both major parties and by the bureaucrats whose cosy habits it would threaten. Without something of the kind, however, I do not believe that the juggernaut which David Howell, John Pardoe and I have all, in different ways, tried to describe can ever be brought under anything that can realistically be described as democratic control.

6. Political Pressures and Democratic Institutions

JOHN PARDOE

THE AUTHOR

JOHN PARDOE was born in 1934 and educated at Sherborne and Corpus Christi College, Cambridge (MA). He has been Liberal MP for Cornwall North since 1966, Treasurer of the Liberal Party, 1968-69, and is Liberal Party Shadow Chancellor of the Exchequer. He is married with three children.

There is scope for endless debate about the economic effects of a high level of government expenditure. The article by David Smith in the *National Westminster Bank Quarterly Review* (November 1975) was an extremely skilful analysis of the factors involved. After a detailed international comparison, he concludes first that, over the long run, inflation does not appear to be related to the magnitude of current public expenditure and, second, that the volume of gross capital formation does appear to be adversely affected by increased public consumption. Indeed, he says, increased public consumption takes place almost entirely at the expense of investment, and that that affects the growth rate.

What is not shown by these international comparisons, or indeed any others I have been able to find, is that Britain spends a higher proportion of her national disposable income in the public sector than do other countries: certainly not in 1972. Total public current expenditure, excluding transfer payments, as a proportion of national disposable income in 1972, in the UK was 20·7 per cent, in Canada 22·4, Denmark 23·8, West Germany 20·4, Sweden 25·6, USA 23·2. You may say I have selected those conveniently in the same part of the league table as Great Britain, and that is true. But it is impossible to conclude from these figures that our long-term economic problems, which are substantially worse than those countries I have mentioned, are due to our high level of public expenditure.

Nor is it true to say that the increase in the percentage of the national disposable income spent in the public sector over the last decade in the UK has been larger than in other countries. Between 1961 and 1972 this percentage in the UK went up by 2·7 per cent, in Canada by 4·4 per cent, in Denmark by 8·9 per cent, in West Germany by 4·9 per cent, in Sweden by 8·1 per cent and in the USA by 2.3 per cent. Perhaps 1972 is not a typical year; the increase in the UK has been very substantial since then. But then it has been pretty substantial elsewhere, although we do not have very exact figures. In any event the UK's economic problems did not begin after 1972, and therefore it does not seem to me one can say that the volume of public expenditure is the principal cause of these long-term problems.

I am making no value-judgements about public expenditure. I do not assume it is bad. Perhaps I am the only person in this room who requires that proposition to be proved to me. Nor do I *know* certainly what the results of reducing public expenditure would be. Which of the other constitutents of demand would benefit if we were to reduce public expenditure? Would it be personal consumption, or productive investment, or exports?

I accept that there is a close link between high public expenditure and low productive investment. That link is proved in the David Smith article. But is it a cause-and-effect link? And, if it is, which is cause and which is effect? I admit that, in all countries, when public expenditure goes up, productive investment goes down. But it may well be that public expenditure goes up *because* productive investment goes down.

So you see that on the theology of public expenditure I am an agnostic. However, some views I do accept. I accept Rudolf Klein's statement[1] that

'The increasing proportion of the gross domestic product spent by the government is . . . not so much a measure of the economic impact of public expenditure as of political and social change. A society where the government of the day determines the distribution of nearly one-half of its total resources is different from one where it controls only a third or less.'

Obviously that is true. Obviously that society is different. However it does not necessarily mean that its economic performance is less because that change has taken place.

I accept that public expenditure has increased both in real terms and as a proportion of the gross domestic product. The record is splendidly set out in an article by Cedric Sandford and Ann Robinson in the November issue of *The Banker*, which also explores the reasons for the failure of political control over public expenditure. I accept too that some of the increased public expenditure has been unnecessary, inefficient and wasteful. I also accept that the public sector borrowing requirement is becoming impossible to finance without inflation of the money supply; and that increasing taxes to meet the expenditure is even more impossible. If one takes the estimated borrowing requirement of £9,000 million (and that was only the estimated one!), it was equal to the total estimated revenue this year from all consumption taxes, and compares with taxes on income, both

---

[1] In *Inflation and Priorities*, published by the Centre for Studies in Social Policy, London, 1975, p. 13.

corporate and individual, of £17,000 million. In order to close the gap you have got to do a lot of taxing to make any impression at all.

'A degree of inevitability'

Why has this happened? We must analyse some of the forces that have made it happen to see whether they are likely to continue to exercise their sway; whether they can be resisted; how far we are going to have to live with increasing public expenditure; and how we can ensure that it is spent wisely and well.

Rudolf Klein says:

'Looking at the trends of the past 20 years, the first conclusion would certainly appear to be that the rise of public expenditure is irresistible. Governments of different political parties have come and gone; some sternly proclaiming the virtues of economy and others dedicated to a policy of increased spending. But expenditure has continued on its upward path, although that path has been steeper for local than for central government spending, and for current rather than capital expenditure . . . it is difficult to avoid the conclusion that public expenditure is partly generated by public services and partly reflects the changing condition of society: that it is out of control not in a technical but in a more fundamental sense'.[2]

That is absolutely right, and I am not sure I see too much hope of reducing the total of public expenditure in the long run, though I suspect that some effort will be made to reduce it in the short term.

Admittedly Klein qualifies the impression of inevitability; but nevertheless there is a degree of inevitability which we have to take into account.

Why does it happen? I must tell you quite frankly that the first reason is that people want it to happen. They ask for it to happen. Never a day goes by without my constituents writing at least half a dozen letters devising new ways of spending more public money. I think it was Enoch Powell who said 'Democracy is inflationary'. My constituents constantly ask me to spend money, and they do not think of it as their money; and, to be quite honest, I do not always think of it as mine. And so it goes on being spent.

Moreover, since there appears to be no rational system of allocating the loot, it depends on who shouts the loudest. Now I am rather

---

[2] *Ibid.*, pp. 11-13.

good at shouting loud (at least my constituents appear to think so), and, since I rely on their good opinion of me to return me to Parliament, I shall continue to shout loud. I have no doubt that the other 629 will do so also.

Every MP shouts as loud as he can in order to be heard above the din. Of course high taxation may eventually bring about some constraint. It is beginning to tell at last. Indeed, I have good news for you: even in the depths of Cornwall, there are those who are feeling the pinch. Ten years ago no-one at the lower end of the income scale ever came in with their pay slip and said: 'It's disgraceful—look how much is being removed from my pay packet'. Because of course 10 years ago the average person did not have much removed from his pay packet. But now he has a substantial amount removed from his pay packet, and once he gets into that bracket where he has anything removed at all, he knows that it is 35 per cent of every pound thereafter. And that's a good whack for anybody to have to put up with.

The trouble is that taxation and expenditure are seen both by parliament and people as very different. They are very rarely debated together. It is almost impossible to get them debated together, in the House of Commons, either in Committee or in the Chamber itself.

Take, for example, the cost of making up private roads. I do my best, as a good representative of the national interest, to explain to people that they cannot expect the ratepayers generally to put up the money for this. 'You are the frontagers', I say, 'the value of your property will go up if this road is made up.' But do you think that explanation ever gets through? Not a bit. I have done it, I suppose, on a dozen occasions in the last two years, and I am aware of a totally bewildered and pained expression on the faces of those I am addressing. I do not believe I am getting through. It is a somewhat despairing situation to be in, but if you can give me some better arguments I will use them.

The government spending establishment

Added to the general pressure for more public expenditure there is, of course, the growing particular pressure of what I would call the public spending establishment: the Civil Service, the local government officers, etc. All of them (and there are masses more now than ever before)—they are all there, with their hand in the till. They are only too anxious, not only to increase their salaries (they have done that remarkably effectively; I wish I had increased mine like they have), but also to spend more and more money because their jobs depend on spending more and more money.

And take civil servants' pensions and salaries. Why have we to pay our top civil servants so much more than other European countries pay theirs? If you read the report of the Boyle Committee on Civil Service Salaries, you will not actually find the details in the text, because Lord Boyle has a very great respect for public servants. But if you look at the back you will find three very significant tables. If you put them together you can find some dramatic stuff. First of all, they show what, say, a Permanent Secretary was paid in this country in 1972 (when the figure was round about £16,000) and what his equivalent was paid in France, Germany, Holland, etc. Then if you turn the page over you find a very helpful table which shows what a typical senior executive (a Managing Director, say) of a very large private company in these various countries was paid. Then you turn over the page again and you find another helpful table which enables you to work out what their post-tax income was. And when you put them all together you come up with some astonishing figures. In France it is necessary to pay the equivalent of a Permanent Secretary only 39 per cent of the net post-tax salary of a typical chief executive. In Belgium the figure is 43 per cent, in Italy 46 per cent, in Germany 58 per cent, in the Netherlands 65 per cent; but in the UK it is 84 per cent. Why? In 1973 the equivalent grade of a Permanent Secretary in Belgium was paid £9,800, in France £9,600, in Italy £9,000, in the Netherlands £12,000, in Germany £14,500, and in the UK £15,900. Who agreed to that? Who fixed it? None other than the Civil Service Public Expenditure Establishment.

I have tried to find out in recent weeks how much of the increase in public expenditure has been due to increases in salaries. It is a very difficult figure to calculate because the Treasury is determined not to let you and me know. In answer to a letter of mine last April, Joel Barnet, Chief Financial Secretary, told me that out of the total public expenditure increases between 1973-74 and 1974-75 of about £10,000 million, £2,500 million was accounted for by wage and salary increases. But of course that is not the whole story, because a lot of the increases in public expenditure went in subsidies to the nationalised industries; and their salary increases are not included in that figure of £2,500 million, though of course such salary increases helped to create the subsidy.

Again, in answer to a parliamentary question recently, in which I tried to elicit further information, I received another evasive reply. I asked him:

'By how much the expenditure by the Consolidated Fund rose during the months of 1975 for which figures are available, and if he will estimate how much of this increase was due to pay increases in the public sector above those allowable under the restrictive legislation of the Social Contract?'

This was the quite delightful reply he gave me:

'As regards the last part of the question, the Government have ensured that all settlements to which they have been a party have been consistent with the Social Contract.'

Now you know, and I know, that this is nonsense. First of all, it is directly counter to Wynne Godley[3] and therefore must by definition be nonsense. And, secondly, there are some problems with the figures. Because if the increase in total Consolidated Fund Expenditure is 47 per cent as a whole—that is the total—and yet the pay element kept within the Social Contract—say, within 20 per cent because that's roughly the rise in the cost of living over the period—the rest of it must have gone up enormously. So there is something missing in the figures and I hope if we go on pressing we may even find out what.

The expenditure community

There is also the 'Expenditure Community' which is so delightfully revealed in a magnificent book I recommend to all, *The Private Government of Public Money*, by Hugh Heclo and Aaron Wildavsky.[4]

To give you some taste of what the book is all about, here is a quote from a Principal Finance Officer:

'Ministers are always in a dilemma. The public policy of their party requires restraint in spending but their political future depends on spending.'[5]

---

[3] Evidence to House of Commons Expenditure Committee (General Sub-Committee), 6 November, 1975.

[4] Macmillan, London, 1974. There is enormous source material here for a whole range of political novels I shall write when I have lost my seat.

[5] *Ibid.,* p. 129.

And the authors have this to say:

> 'Inside his department, the spending minister who is uninterested in increased spending is likely to be viewed, if not with distaste, at least with despair.'[6]

So the pressures upon a Minister are immense. When the last Conservative Government came to power we had cuts in school milk and things like that. Heclo and Wildavsky comment thus:

> 'The tendency [to spend] was put to the test in 1970. Few governments can have started out more devoted to government economy than the Conservatives, with their business-minded reforms in education: charges for school meals and an ending of free school milk. But a year later the economising Minister of Education, like other Conservative spending ministers, could be found in the usual political operation of commending herself to a client audience by citing increased spending.'[7]

One marvellous instance of this whole nonsense was the debate about the raising of the school-leaving age. Nobody was ever able to prove that raising the school-leaving age would add one jot or tittle to the quality of education. Almost alone in the House of Commons ever since 1966 when I was my party's spokesman on education, I challenged the whole basis on which the school-leaving age was being raised. In particular I alleged that we did not have the resources to do it and that it was crazy to spread them so thinly across the field. I remember telling Sir Edward Boyle, as he then was, that he really should stop waving this radical flag. Because that's all it was. It was just a rather nasty gesture—because if one did not wave it one was thought to be reactionary. But, alas, it went through, and the reason is of course that Secretaries of State need something in the history books. It is no good having a paragraph in a history book which says that so and so increased the quality of education during his/her period of office, because that is impossible to prove. So you have to have a paragraph that says: 'During Mrs Margaret Thatcher's period of office the school-leaving age was raised, or primary schools were improved', or some ludicrous nonsense like that. Improved?—what does improving primary school education mean? It means what she said in 1971 when she

[6] *Ibid.*, p. 135.
[7] *Ibid.*, pp. 135-36.

promised that 'within five years we'll be within sight of replacing all the pre-1903 primary schools'. 70 per cent of the primary schools in Cornwall are pre-1903! And there's nothing wrong with most of them at all. It would be an absolute scandal to replace them—it would be a damnable waste of public money. Of course, it was a total fantasy. We won't replace them, thank goodness—and I'm very glad we won't.

So there it is. Those are the sort of pressures that are building up, and frankly I do not expect to see a countervailing force asserted in my lifetime.

Frequent change of government

Another major influence on public expenditure is the constant change in government. Nothing ever stays still. British government never takes that marvellous advice Adlai Stevenson gave to Eisenhower: 'Don't just do something; stand there!' Every government that comes in changes everything the previous one did. Just look at the list of changes in investment incentives. My colleague in the House of Lords, Lady Seear, quoted some of them yesterday in a speech—not all because there have been over 90 significant changes in the investment incentives in the last 10 years. With what effect? That major public companies have sent their executives to House of Commons Select Committees to tell us these items change so often that they no longer bother to feed them into the computers on which they calculate their investment plans. So here we all are, spending vast sums of money, trying to persuade people in industry to invest, and they do not even bother to take account of them in their investment plans because they change so often!

You are not going to change that situation unless you change the political settlement—unless you scrap the two-party dog fight where every party comes in determined only to undo what the previous one has done. The best thing that could happen if a Liberal government got elected next time would be a Queen's speech in which she stood up and said: 'My Lords and members of the House of Commons, my government proposes to do absolutely nothing for five years. God bless you all.'

There are no constraints on expenditure in government or in the Civil Service—quite the opposite. There are no constraints on expenditure in parliament—quite the opposite. There are no constraints on expenditure in local government—quite the opposite.

And expenditure will go on increasing however many seminars you hold or whatever I or you say. There are remedies one can propose, many of them very helpfully set out in Cedric Sandford's article. I have argued that indexation of the tax system would introduce some constraint because at least it would ensure that the Chancellor could not by-pass whatever parliamentary controls there are. But public expenditure will continue to increase. What we have to do is not only to try to develop constraints—that is useful but will not be very effective—but to ensure that the expenditure is well spent—as efficiently as it would be if it were spent in the private sector. And that is a very, very difficult task indeed.

A Case Study:
How Effective is Expenditure on Education?

RICHARD LYNN

Professor of Psychology, The New University of Ulster

THE AUTHOR

RICHARD LYNN was educated at King's College, Cambridge. Lecturer in Psychology at the University of Exeter, 1956 to 1967. Research Professor of Psychology at the Economic & Social Research Institute, Dublin, 1967 to 1971. Professor of Psychology at the New University of Ulster since 1972.

Those who advocate cutting government expenditure are frequently asked for precise details of the services they would axe. This has often proved to be a difficult question because no-one wishes to adopt the mantle of hatchet-man of the poor, the sick, the elderly, and so forth. Nevertheless we should consider in detail sectors of government expenditure with a view to evaluating exactly what return the public is getting for its money.

To further this examination I shall consider the return from government expenditure on education, a rapidly growing item. As a percentage of GNP government expenditure on education stood at 3·1 per cent in 1950 and had grown to 6·5 per cent by 1973. There are now approximately $1\frac{1}{2}$ million employees in education; even in the years from 1970 to the present this number expanded by about 20 per cent.

Does education increase economic growth?

The first question is: What is the justification for these rising sums of expenditure? Three main answers have been given. The first is that it will constitute an investment for economic growth. This view was fairly popular in the 1950s and received some kind of official endorsement in the 1959 Crowther Report on the education of young people in late adolescence, and also in the Robbins Report. But support for this thesis has waned over the 1960s and 70s. It is certainly by no means definitively established, and indeed in the view of many people is not even plausible.

There are two chief reasons for the waning of support for the thesis. One is that there are no consistent differences in expenditure on education between nations with fast and slow economic growth, and certainly the United Kingdom does not spend less on education than many countries with faster rates of economic growth. Second, doubts have arisen about the causes underlying the association between education and earnings. People who have had a lot of education tend to earn high incomes, and some economists assumed that this was cause and effect. More recently psychologists and sociologists have found that education as such has little effect on cognitive ability and have been led to the conclusion that other factors associated with education, particularly intelligence and home background, are the main causes of the apparent relation between education and earnings.

This conclusion has been put most fully by Professor Christopher Jencks in his book *Inequality* (1973). As a result many economists have revised their opinion on the significance of education as an investment for economic growth. This change of view has been expressed, for instance, by Professor John Vaizey in his book, *The Political Economy of Education* (1972).

A second argument for increasing public expenditure on education is that it will raise the general level of intelligence, intellectual competence, flexibility and so forth of its recipients, and they will therefore be a more efficient labour force and a more efficient population generally.

Thirdly, there is rather an important special case of this argument: that increasing expenditure on education will help to break the poverty and deprivation cycle in which children brought up in deprived, poor, 'under-privileged' families tend to do poorly at school and become themselves poor, 'under-privileged' families, so that the cycle is perpetuated down the generations. It has been hoped that we can break this cycle by spending more on the education of these children, so lifting them out of the cycle of poverty.

My own view is that none of these three arguments is sufficiently well established to justify this rising expenditure. This conclusion is largely derived from the studies of the effects of educational expenditures on the cognitive abilities of the pupils.

Nursery education

It is convenient to consider the question in terms of the various age groups who are receiving education and to start with the youngest, that is, young children of three to five who receive nursery school education. This is at the moment the most fashionable area for expansion: a commitment to increase the provision of nursery schools was included in the Labour Party Manifesto of 1974. This programme has particularly been adopted because of the hopes that it will break the poverty cycle. If we give children from poor homes accelerated extra education before they go to junior schools they will be at a relative advantage in competition with middle-class children and so improve their skills and general position in society.

There have been many studies on the effectiveness of nursery school education. By 1939 nine studies had been carried out. They all produced the same result. They showed that nursery school education sometimes has some temporary effect in raising the educational attainments of the children but that it has invariably disappeared by the time the child is eight or nine. Since the war numerous investigations, running into literally dozens of studies of this kind, have been done and the results have confirmed the pre-war studies. They are absolutely clear and unequivocal that nursery school education has no measurable effect on the educational abilities of the children who receive them. Arthur Jensen began his famous article in 1969 in the *Harvard Educational Review:* 'Compensatory education has been tried and it apparently has failed'. Nevertheless one of the lessons from this sector of government expenditure is that, even though the weight of empirical evidence can become solid and strong, those who advocate increasing expenditure are remarkably blind to it. So in 1966 the report of the Plowden Committee advocated the extension of nursery schooling in Britain in the hope that it would improve the cognitive skills of young children.

Nursery schooling expenditure has increased around four-fold from 1960 to the present, though it is only around £9 million a year. It should be nipped in the bud before it becomes substantial, as it clearly has the potential to do. I would suggest that the evidence indicates that nursery schooling is essentially a service in the same way that a launderette is a service to parents of young families, and it should be priced accordingly.

Is compulsory education effective?

On the effectiveness of compulsory schooling between five and 15 or 16 our main sources of evidence come from comparisons of one school with another. The first major study in Britain on this question was carried out in the early 1950s by L. C. D. Kemp. He took 50 London schools and tested the intelligence and educational attainments in reading, arithmetic and spelling of 10-year-old children and related their standards of attainment to a number of variables in the school. Particularly interesting are the staff-pupil ratio and the quality of the buildings. Kemp found there was no relationship at all between the attainments of school children and favourability of the staff-pupil ratio or the newness of the buildings.

These two items are particularly important because they are areas of expenditure in education which have grown substantially over the last quarter-century. The teacher-pupil ratio has dropped by about 10 per cent leading to the employment of many thousands more teachers. And many new buildings have been put up and old ones torn down.

The second study in Britain along the same lines was made by Professor F. W. Warburton in the city of Salford in 1960. He investigated the relationship between the attainments of the children in all the secondary modern schools in Salford and the size of the class and the newness of the buildings. Once again there was no significant relationship.

Many more studies have been done in the United States and here we have to draw the conclusion that even private enterprise cannot raise the educational skills of school children. Over the last decade or so experiments have been carried out in 'performance contracting': a local school authority puts the task of raising the educational attainments of backward children out for tender. The purpose is to raise their attainment by, say, a year of educational growth in six months. The firms unlucky enough to win these contracts have called in all manner of psychological and educational experts to assist in raising educational achievement. All the latest methods have been used, including visual aids, trading stamps as rewards, individual attention and teaching machines. The results have been disappointing. Most of the firms are now out of business and the United States Office of Educational Opportunity has itself concluded that the experiments have been a failure.

US experience negative

Because of its wider social and cultural variability than in Britain, the United States is a good place to study the effects of expenditure on education and its results in the achievements of children. In New York, for example, the expenditure per child is about two and a half times that in the Southern States, and yet children in New York, when you allow for their intelligence and the socio-economic background of their parents, do no better in educational tests than children in the Southern States. This question has been well reviewed by Professor Christopher Jencks. He reached this conclusion:

> 'We can see no evidence that either school administrators or educational experts know how to raise test scores even when they have vast resources at their disposal'.

Jencks's conclusion is a particularly interesting one because he is not a crusty reactionary who dislikes increasing government expenditure. He is a committed egalitarian who is in effect saying to his fellow egalitarians: this view, which we egalitarians have had, that if we pour more money into education we are going to make a more equal society, is a *cul-de-sac*. The best thing to do, if you want a more equal society, is to tax the middle class and redistribute the proceeds to the poor *in cash*. That is the essential message of Jencks's book.

Thus studies in both Britain and the United States point to the conclusion that increasing expenditure on education for the 5-16 year age group does not raise standards. This does not necessarily mean that education has *no* effect on children, and it may be that dedicated, enthusiastic and intelligent teachers produce good results. What it does suggest is that we do not get better quality teaching *simply* by increasing the numbers of teachers, building new schools or providing more ancilliary help.

15 plus

The next age group is the 15-year-olds. I would like to dwell on them particularly because they were the group affected by raising the school-leaving age in 1972 from 15 to 16. As a result something of the order of 350,000 15-year-olds were obliged to stay at school who had previously been allowed to enter employment. This measure involved a substantial increase in expenditure for which there is, I suggest, very little justification.

First, there is no solid reason either on economic or psychological grounds to suppose that coercing these young people to remain in school will yield any benefits to society. Secondly, compulsory schooling for 15-year-olds is an affront to the principle of personal liberty that people should be allowed to conduct their lives as they wish so long as they do not damage others, which is hardly true of adolescents of 15 who wish to leave school and take employment. Thirdly, there are social costs in forcing adolescents to remain at school. What would one imagine on commonsense grounds would happen if adolescents who do not wish to be at school were compelled to stay there, or at any rate if it were made illegal for them to take employment or for employers to employ them? You would expect many of them to play truant. They are going to be without money, bored at school, and so some will take to crime. That expectation was documented in the Crowther Report when the school-leaving age was last raised in 1947-48. There was a jump in the crime rate of the 14-year-olds, and the same thing occurred in 1973 when the government obliged 15-year-olds to remain in school: their crime rate jumped approximately 5 per cent. My conclusion is that raising the school-leaving age in 1972 was objectionable on several grounds in addition to the increase in expenditure, which is of the order of £150 million a year.

Conclusion on education expenditure: no measurable return

To summarise: I have taken three stages of schooling, nursery schools for 3-5 year-olds, the increased expenditure of the last quarter-century on children and young adolescents of compulsory school age between 5 and 15, and raising the school-leaving age to 16 in 1972. My conclusion is that there has been no measurable return for the considerable sums spent on these measures. The other side of this coin is that children's educational achievements are very largely determined by their genes and by their family environments; their schools have relatively little effect. I believe there is now fairly general agreement on these conclusions among social scientists.

Now I should like to draw one or two general conclusions from this consideration of the benefits of expenditure on education.

First, we have to recognise that the expansionist propensities of the public sector are so strong that they override empirical evidence which throws doubt on the effectiveness of the expenditure, and this makes the control of expenditure a formidable task for government.

Secondly, I think governments have often made matters worse for themselves by consulting experts about whether their province should be expanded. This has happened again and again in education. The sequence is this: there is public discussion about whether we should expand this sector. Should we have more universities? Or raise the school-leaving age? Or have nursery schools? The government then appoints a committee to consider the question and man it with people employed either in the sector itself or in related sectors. So if you wish to find out and receive informed opinion about whether the school-leaving age should be raised, as was done with the Crowther Report, the people appointed to the committee are headmasters and HMI's and Professors of Education and educational training officers in firms and so forth. Finally, the predictable report is made: yes, the sector should be expanded. The government is now lumbered with this report and under pressure to implement it, which in due course it does. That is a very familiar sequence.

Thirdly, is the strength of public pressure for expanded services really as powerful as is often supposed? Quite commonly there is very little real public support for expansion of the service. We have no better example than the raising of the school-leaving age in 1972-73. We know the great bulk of teachers were against it. Polls of teachers' views from the late 1960s onwards showed that something of the order of 70 to 80 per cent of teachers thought that raising the school-leaving age would be a mistake. There was a Schools Council inquiry by Miss Morton Williams published in 1968 which reported the opinions of some thousands of adolescents, of 20-year-olds, and of parents of school children which showed widespread antipathy to secondary education of the present academic type, leading in the case of about 50 per cent of the child population to no tangible diplomas or certificates from which they would have something to show for the work they had put in at school. Thus there appears to have been very little support in the general population for the raising of the school-leaving age. We had what I suggest was a very small lobby of activists whom politicians have mistaken for widespread public demand.

In a word: It has been very difficult to demonstrate any measurable benefit from the very large increases in expenditure on education over the last quarter of a century. I suspect this conclusion might be equally applicable to many other parts of government expenditure.

REFERENCES

KEMP, L. C. D., 'Environmental and other characteristics determining attainments in primary schools', *British Journal of Educational Psychology*, 1955, 25, 67-77.

LITTLE, A., 'Do small classes help a pupil?', *New Society*, 21 October, 1971.

MARKLUND, S., 'Scholastic attainment as related to size and homogeneity of classes', in A. Yates (ed.), *Grouping in Education*, UNESCO, 1966.

MORRIS, J. M., *Standards and Progress in Reading,* National Foundation for Educational Research, 1966.

MORTON WILLIAMS, R., and FINCH, S., *Young School Leavers,* HMSO, 1968.

WARBURTON, F. W. 'Attainment and the School Environment', in S. Wiseman (ed.), *Education and Environment*, Manchester University Press, 1964.

JENCKS, Christopher, *Inequality: a re-assessment of the effect of family and schooling in America,* Basic Books, New York, and Allan Lane, London, 1973.

VAIZEY, John, *The Political Economy of Education*, Duckworth, 1972.

Crowther Report, *15 to 18*, Vols. 1 and 2: Report of the Central Advisory Council (England), HMSO, London, 1959, 1960.

Plowden Report, *Children and their Primary Schools,* Vol. 1 (Report) and Vol. 2 (Appendices): Report of the Central Advisory Council (England), HMSO, London, 1967.

Robbins Report, *Report of the Committee on Higher Education*, Cmnd. 2154, HMSO, London, 1963.

From the Floor

A selection of contributions to the discussion of the Seminar papers, in alphabetical order

RONALD HALSTEAD (*Chairman of Beecham Products*): We in industry put to the Conservative Government when they introduced the price code that it would depress profits very substantially, by weakening our cash flow and making it impossible for us to invest. And it happened pretty well exactly as we said. We also repeated this to eminent economists like Shirley Williams and the present Treasury officials.

What is the economist's justification for a prices code that, for example, destroys the investment incentive of the food industry for a reduction of a half per cent on the Retail Price Index? The Retail Price Index has been rising at 26 or 27 per cent a year. The difference between $26\frac{1}{2}$ and 27 in terms of bargaining power with the unions is neither here nor there. So what is the economic justification?

Nationalised industries' rate of return

RALPH HARRIS (*Gen. Director, IEA*): George Polanyi, whom we miss a great deal, in a study[1] over a long period of years from the 1950s right through to the 1970s, examined the rate of return in the state sector against the manufacturing private sector. He showed that the average rate of return of the nationalised industries was less than one-third that of private industry. He then brought in the complication mentioned by Mr Eltis that periodic instructions were given by their political masters to hold down prices, thereby distorting the commercial rate of return. Mr Polanyi showed that over the period covered by his comparisons, the rate of increase in prices in the state sector was certainly not less than in the private sector.

*   *   *

CHRISTOPHER MEAKIN (*Director, Home Affairs, Association of British Chambers of Commerce*): I was interested in Professor Wilson's idea of putting a direct question on allocation of resources to the taxpayer on his tax-form. There is a direct parallel in the

---

[1] *Comparative Returns from Investment in Nationalised Industries*, Background Memorandum No. 1, IEA, 1968.

United States, where the whole process of local and regional government has a very commonplace system known as propositions. By a very small quorum some tens of thousands of electors can put any question they like on the ballot form at local government elections, and the voting is binding on the legislature. They typically tend to be questions on resource allocation: school programmes, public works, and so on.

Profits and savings in Japan

CHRISTOPHER MEAKIN: In the Japanese economy—with its enormous rate of growth—the corporate sector generally speaking has a chronically low rate of profit. The other curious feature of the Japanese economy is that the private sector has a phenomenally high propensity to save. Between these two you get a very high rate of growth which would indicate a very high rate of recycling savings back into investment.

*   *   *

BRIAN READING (*Economics Editor, The Economist*): The salient factor about the Japanese economy is the very low proportion of public expenditure to national income. That takes one through the route by which the money gets from savings into the company sector. In Japan there has to be a very high level of personal savings because there aren't social security benefits and there is a very underdeveloped financial system for personal savings. The result is something like 20 to 25 per cent personal savings put into financial assets, which pay around 2 per cent. That money is then channelled through their financial system into the company sector and hence provides the subsidised funds for the investor. In Britain we are seeing at the moment not merely that investment is being depressed but that personal savings are considerably increased. It's possible the savings schedule has changed its position—this we won't know until we see whether or not it changes back when inflation slows down.

The financial institutions through whom virtually all the savings go rather than direct to the government are getting caught in precisely the same dilemma that the companies get caught on their gearing. It is not merely that companies find it difficult to borrow; it is increasingly difficult for any financial institution to lend to the company sector. They are forced therefore to channel the money into the public sector, which at this stage in the cycle goes to finance public consumption. At a later stage, if company profits do not improve, it will form the basis for subsidised lending to companies through the government. The government therefore takes over the role of doling out the money and taking over the rest, and this is the way the system looks likely to develop unless there is an increase in profitability.

Statistics, preferences and polls

BRIAN READING: There are two extremes. On one side you have the politicians saying that as far as they know people want this, people want that. The other side says that in order to discover what people want we have to have the market system, the token [voucher] system. Part of the evidence on the question of raising the school-leaving age was a poll among teachers. It is extraordinary that although a massive amount of statistics are collected very little seems to be about precisely what people want. Why don't we say: 'We are going to raise the school-leaving age, we will have an official poll on it'? This is a quick halfway house between the market system and the pressure-group, and I think it could be achieved very easily, very cheaply and very quickly.

Quantity versus quality in education

GORDON RICHARDS (*Senior Lecturer in Government, West London College*): I spent 13 years as a Labour Member of various local authorities, including three years as chairman of a London Borough Education Committee.

The time has come, as Professor Lynn has indicated, to de-sanctify education. We tend to speak of education in rather hushed, reverent tones. I would like to see it put in the market-place and sold as a commodity as between a willing buyer and a willing seller. We would get much better education, and we would save a great deal of money.

The myth is steadily fostered that in some way state education is starved of resources whereas the private sector has unlimited resources. A few months ago I got from my local authority the *per capita* cost of education. This is an outer London Borough, composed to a large extent of the 'under-privileged'. We find that the *per capita* cost of nursery schooling, for instance, is £595. I think a private enterprise school could do a lot with that, and a lot more effectively.

Primary schools cost, *per capita*, £298; secondary schools, £531; residential special schools, £2,290; day special schools, £1,129. I suggest there is very little evidence there of the state sector of education being starved. Yet we still have in the Borough a great deal of discontent with the quality of education. There was, for instance, just over 12 months ago a walk-out of about 200 secondary school pupils on the grounds that the school was understaffed. Yet when I looked into the pupil/teacher ratio I found it was 14·9 pupils to 1. Again, no evidence that they were understaffed. Neither did they lack equipment: it was a new school building from which they walked out. Nor did they come from 'deprived' housing conditions. Most of the areas from which the pupils came have just been rehoused in high-rise Council flats.

So all the indices normally given as excuses to explain misconduct and poor standards did not exist. It is time we disposed of this myth that the state sector in education is under-provided for. It certainly is not in my Borough. Although our figures are slightly above the national average, they confirm that by spending more money you do not necessarily get better results. And, if I may add in passing, I believe that one of the main arguments for the education voucher, particularly the supplemented voucher which a parent could use in the private sector topped up with some of his own resources, is that when a parent puts some of his own money on the table he takes a much closer interest in how it is spent.

It is too easy for councillors and officials to spend other people's money. It is as simple as that. It is said that half of the people now employed in education are not teaching. I can well believe it from my own experience in further education. Here is a happy hunting ground for waste, extravagance and misdirection. Most of the students are day-release and my own students come from local government and the Civil Service. I am not likely to be out of a job for a long time to come! There are plenty of them. These students are not underpaid. I came across a 20-year-old the other day in a Civil Service department who'd managed to fail a very modest exam last year, earning £2,400. They come on full salary; and if you require them to buy textbooks there is never any resistance because they do not pay for them. The taxpayer and the ratepayer do. Up to £20, anyway, which more than covers the requirements of most of their courses. They then have a travel allowance to take account of the difference in the cost of reaching the college rather than going to work, and some of them under the age of 18—there are very few of those—get luncheon vouchers as well. They start the course and then find that it is not quite to their liking and after a term or so they give it up. They do not have to worry about the cost, after all it is free. And this, on a very large scale, is not generally known by the public.

* * *

ANN ROBINSON (*Lecturer in Economics, University College, Cardiff*): In the private sector you buy quality. I am not ashamed to say that I use my entire net income to buy quality education, and I am convinced I am buying the raising of educational attainment. That is, there is a myth somewhere behind the figures on government expenditure. It is possible to spend money and get better grades, better raising of educational attainments. You do not do it by buying quantity, but by buying quality. It is something to do with the people in the school. I went to one of Britain's famous public schools recently on behalf of my son. I was interested to find that the headmaster of one of the Clarendon schools teaches, whereas the local comprehensive headmaster in my town does not teach and neither does 10 per cent of his staff. This is the sort of comparison that has to be made: What is the quality of the education? Could you spend money and get better quality? What do the people in the system do that you are spending the money on? Are you spending money on teaching or on people administering the service? Those are the questions that people should be asking about government spending. What are you getting for the money?

The marketed and non-marketed sectors

IAN SENIOR (*senior consultant, Economists Advisory Group*): Mr Eltis's distinction between the marketed and non-marketed sectors of the economy is very valuable but in certain respects it is too broad and possibly misleading. If a builder's labourer transfers from a private company to the direct labour department of a local authority, he is in practice working at the same job, but this would distort the equation. I disagree with Mr Eltis's argument that each transfer of a productive worker from the marketed to the non-marketed sector produces a double effect. If, for example, a building worker transfers and becomes a civil servant the amount of his productive output is certainly lost but his expectation of purchasing television sets, etc., is in no way increased, except in so far as state sector salaries, as it now appears, are substantially higher than those in the private sector. To that extent a transfer from the marketed to the non-marketed sector does impose a further burden on demand and resources.

Practicability of cutting government expenditure

BRENDON SEWILL (*Special Assistant to the Chancellor of the Exchequer, 1970-74*): One of the reasons why public expenditure has gone up so much in the last ten years is that it has been based on much too optimistic assumptions about the rate of growth in the economy. Because we haven't had the growth public expenditure has continued to go up as a percentage of GNP.

What do we do about efficiency in government? I'm not sure that all the innovations the last government introduced have solved the problem. I remember that both political parties supported the reform of local government because it was going to increase the efficiency of local government! The main problem is that throughout the whole Civil Service and local government there is practically no incentive to cut manpower or costs. All the incentive is to increase the size of their bureaux. We should set up a three-man economies tribunal, somewhat like the Ombudsman, that would take suggestions both from the public and from people inside the Civil Service on how public expenditure could be reduced. If this was put into effect and found effective, the person who suggested it should be awarded half the saving in the first year tax free. I think this could be quite effective.

How does one cut in practice? I was involved in the 1970 exercise and I regret to say we were rather unscientific about it. A few of us got together and went through the estimates and made a list of the things we didn't like. Ian Macleod and a couple of MPs in the House of Commons did the same thing and we put them together into a consolidated list. When Ian Macleod became Chancellor he asked me to send him the list. It did not take very long to get translated into action. Three months later there were cuts of £1,600 million. One of our suggestions was the economies tribunal and I've rather regretted that it hadn't been put into effect previously.

One cannot really say that increases in public expenditure are the cause of recent cost-push pressures. In 1970 there were substantial cuts in public expenditure. For three years there were substantial reductions in taxation. It is not higher taxation which has caused all the cost-push inflation. Tremendous pressure was built up against the economies. Recall the changes in the arrangements for the housing subsidies, perhaps the largest cut in public expenditure. The pressure built up, going right through to Clay Cross, was enormous. Exactly the same was true for museum charges. Members of Parliament have to win elections. Where might one cut expenditure? If you abolish the food subsidies and the housing subsidies, you save £1,300 million. And what follows? Absolutely no hope of the unions sticking to the £6 limit. Many people think that incomes policy is no use, but if the pay claims came in at twice the rate of £6 public expenditure would be vastly increased again. Drastic cuts in Civil Service manpower? One of the biggest places where this could be done is in the Overseas Diplomatic Service. It is now three times as big as pre-war but this country has only a third of the overseas influence. If you cut overseas embassies back to the pre-war level, you save £60 million. Abolish overseas information: save £50 million. Halve the present rate of motorway construction: £150 million. Increase the charges for school meals from 15p to the full cost 25p: £160 million. Make unemployment and sickness benefit taxable and unions responsible for strike pay: £150 million. What do you get out of all this? Only £500 million.

So what do you do? If you put women's pension age up to 65 you get a storm of protest. It saves you another £500 million. So out of all that you save £1,000 million: only about a tenth of what the borrowing requirement will be this year. And you have stirred up such a storm of public protest and trade union protest that your situation will be far more difficult.

*   *   *

I would confirm what Professor Wilson was hinting at—the doubt about government expenditure being a direct cause of inflation. In practice the power of the unions to push up pay and prices is also the same power that pushes up public expenditure. From my experience in the Treasury, once there was an incomes policy there was also very severe pressure, first of all, to cancel the economies in progress (the rent increases and the increases in school meals were cancelled because they were not consistent with the incomes policy), and secondly, without being too indiscreet, to avoid putting up taxation. Hence on both sides of the equation you get an increase in the public sector borrowing requirement because of the need to maintain an incomes policy. There are two conclusions: either you do away with the incomes policy and have a much tougher monetary policy, or you do something about the trade unions—but that's a different subject.

*   *   *

I cast my vote in favour of floating the pound, but there is no doubt that it has removed a discipline. There is nothing like a really good crisis to concentrate the minds of the Cabinet. Perhaps the moral is not to take economic fashions too seriously, because after all many people thought floating was going to solve all our problems.

The purpose of private enterprise

GERALD THOMPSON (*formerly of Kleinwort Benson*): In the corporate sector—the private sector—the purpose of all enterprise is to create value, market-measured value, in excess of the value of the elements used to create it. It is not to create employment, which is a political objective. If the private sector succeeds in creating more value than it uses it will in practice provide employment and taxation. If it does not it will very soon cease to do either. That is not its objective. The other point is in connection with public sector capital investment where I think one must distinguish very carefully between economic investment and amenity or cultural investment. The point which Mr Eltis makes about the return on measurable public sector capital investment, that is to say, power stations, electricity, gas, etc., is very important but it depends on what they are allowed to charge for their product. But of course beside them one has got to range up the immense investment in unquantifiable capital formations— schools, hospitals, housing, roads—and descending to all kinds of amenity investment, that is to say, substantial investments in loss-making enterprises. The cost of that is not quantifiable but it is obviously enormous.

Malinvestment, macro-forecasts, and pricing

JOHN B. WOOD (*IEA*): There has been gross maldistribution of most or a large chunk of our investment programme since the end

of the war. The initial misinvestment has taken place in such industries as atomic energy and to some extent electricity generation.
Yesterday we saw the outcome of the state decisions on the alumi-
nium smelters, etc. There are innumerable examples. That is the
substantial point. In the state sector the general rate of return on
investment has been, for practical purposes, nil. And of course it
has mopped up a large proportion of such investible funds as the
country has been able to generate.

*   *   *

The discussion has been largely set in the context of that notorious
exercise in national bookkeeping called the Blue Book of Income and
Expenditure, supported by the no less unsatisfactory exercise in
astrology known as forecasts of public expenditure. So much of our
discussion has been in macro terms. This is rather unfortunate,
because if you try to think in terms of individual sectors of the
economy and the provision of particular services or goods and the
degree of political interference, which after all implies government
spending, you come across government activities which are not
supplying a satisfactory service to the public and yet are costing a
bomb. Education, health and housing are three. We need to recast
our whole thinking on them towards introducing a system of
charging, which would imply a substantial saving in public funds.

If you add the industrial subsidies, foreign aid, and the regional
programme, you arrive at an order of magnitude that is, I would
have thought, approximately the same as the budgeted borrowing
requirement. If we are going to try to get some movement in policy
on government spending and inflation, this kind of approach might
be more fruitful.

STATISTICAL APPENDIX

The Growth of Government Expenditure

___

I. GNP AND TOTAL GOVERNMENT EXPENDITURE, 1960-74

		1960	*1965*	*1970*	*1974*	*1975*
						Estimated
GNP	£bn.	22·8	31·7	43·8	74·0	90
Index (1960=100)		100	140	190	325	400
Public Expenditure £bn.		9·4	14·1	21·9	41·6	55
Index (1960=100)		100	150	230	440	580
PE as % of GNP		41·2%	44·6%	50%	56%	61%
Price index (1960=100)		100	116	147	223	280

Increase in GNP at constant prices 1960-74   45%

Increase in PE at constant prices 1960-74   100%

Real increase in PE as proportion of GNP   36%

Source: Blue Books on *National Income and Expenditure* for all Tables.

II. FORMS OF EXPENDITURE

	£ *million*				*Increase*
	1960	*1965*	*1970*	*1974*	*1960=100*
Current goods & services	4,170	6,040	9,090	16,640	400
Fixed capital	1,660	2,780	4,160	6,920	420
Subsidies	500	570	900	2,940	590
Grants to persons	1,650	2,600	4,340	7,850	475
Capital grants	70	180	750	860	1,200
Net lending	90	225	140	1,090	1,200
Overseas grants, etc.	160	240	300	1,060	660
Average increase in PE since 1960					440
Increase in prices since 1960					223

III. MAIN ITEMS OF GOVERNMENT EXPENDITURE

	£ million				Increase in Money terms 1960=100	Real terms
	1960	*1965*	*1970*	*1974*		
Social Services (including housing)	3,910	6,470	10,300	20,430	520	235
Industry & Trade	570	1,015	1,930	3,730	650	290
Defence	1,610	2,130	2,470	4,240	260	115
Transport & Roads	790	1,040	1,740	3,090	390	175
Police & Fire	210	340	630	1,240	590	265
Environment	340	600	1,020	1,865	450	200
Agriculture	320	330	400	1,050	330	150
Debt interest	1,110	1,460	2,145	3,730	340	150
Total	8,860	13,010	20,620	39,370		
% of all PE	94%	92%	94%	94%		

Omitted items: External services, employment services, research, libraries & museums, Parliament, finance and tax collection.

IV. SOCIAL SERVICES EXPENDITURE

	£ million				Increase since 1960
	1960	*1965*	*1970*	*1974*	
					%
Education	920	1,590	2,640	4,860	530
Housing	500	960	1,270	3,940	790
NHS, etc.*	1,000	1,510	2,470	4,780	480
Social Security	1,490	2,410	3,920	6,850	460
Total	3,910	6,470	10,300	20,430	520

*Including personal social services, etc.

V. LOCAL AUTHORITIES: EXPENDITURE AND MAIN SOURCES OF INCOME

	£ million				Increase
	1960	*1965*	*1970*	*1974*	*1960=100*
L.A. expenditure	2,370	4,250	6,990	13,300	560
as % of PE	25%	30%	32%	32%	
L.A. income					
Rates	770	1,230	1,820	2,990	390
Exchequer (current)	780	1,250	2,450	4,820	620
Rents (gross)	320	530	1,000	1,680	525
Borrowing	380	1,030	1,240	3,340	880
	2,250	4,040	6,510	12,830	470

VI. CENTRAL GOVERNMENT CURRENT REVENUE

	£ million				Increase
	1960	*1965*	*1970*	*1974*	*1960=100*
Taxes on income	2,720	4,020	7,420	12,140	450
Taxes on expenditure	2,620	3,730	6,600	8,360	320
N.I. contributions	910	1,680	2,600	4,930	540
Total current revenue	6,820	10,130	17,960	27,600	400

VII. SHIFTS IN UK EMPLOYMENT

Public and Private Sectors: 1956-1974

	(in 000's to nearest 10,000)					Change
	1956	*1960*	*1965*	*1970*	*1974*	*since 1954*
						%
Public Corporations	2,080	1,860	2,020*	2,010	1,940	−7
Central Government:						
H.M. Forces	760	520	420	370	350	−55
Civilian	1,640	1,640	1,370*	1,540	1,750	+6
Local Authorities	1,590	1,740	2,150	2,560	2,830	+78
Total Public	6,070	5,760	5,960	6,480	6,870	+13
Total Private	18,430	19,020	19,240	18,260	18,250	−1
Grand Total	24,500	24,780	25,200	24,740	25,120	+2·5

*Since April 1961 the Post Office (then employing 340,000) is treated as a public corporation instead of part of central government.

(E & O E)

109

IEA READINGS

1. Education—A Framework for Choice
Papers on Historical, Economic and *Administrative Aspects of Choice*
in Education and its Finance
A.C.F. BEALES, MARK BLAUG, E.G. WEST,
SIR DOUGLAS VEALE, *with an Appraisal by* DR RHODES BOYSON
Second Edition, 1970 (xvi+100pp., 50p)

2. Growth through Industry
A re-consideration of principles and *the practice before* and *after the*
National Plan
JOHN JEWKES, JACK WISEMAN, RALPH HARRIS, JOHN BRUNNER,
RICHARD LYNN, and seven company chairmen.
1967 (xiii+157pp., £1·00)

4. Taxation—A Radical Approach
A re-assessment of the high level of British taxation and the means
for its reduction
VITO TANZI, J.B. BRACEWELL-MILNES, D.R. MYDDELTON
1970 (xii+130 pp., 90p)

5. Economic Issues in Immigration
An exploration of the liberal approach to public policy on
immigration
CHARLES WILSON, W.H. HUTT, SUDHA SHENOY, DAVID
COLLARD, E.J. MISHAN, GRAHAM HALLETT, *with an*
Introduction by SIR ARNOLD PLANT.
1970 (xviii+155 pp., £1·25)

7. Verdict on Rent Control
Essays on the economic consequences of political action to restrict
rents in five countries
F.A. HAYEK, MILTON FRIEDMAN and GEORGE J. STIGLER,
BERTRAND DE JOUVENEL, F.W. PAISH, SVEN RYDENFELT, *with an*
Introduction by F. G. PENNANCE.
1972 (xvi+80pp., £1·00)

9. The Long Debate on Poverty
Eight essays on industrialisation and 'the condition of England'
R.M. HARTWELL, G.E. MINGAY, RHODES BOYSON,
NORMAN McCORD, C.G. HANSON, A.W. COATS, W.H. CHALONER
and W.O. HENDERSON, J.M. JEFFERSON.
Second Edition with an introductory essay on 'The State of the Debate' by
NORMAN GASH.
1974 (xxxii+243 pp., £2·50)